The Passionate
Beader's Guide

Best Techniques, Tools & Projects for Beading Success

All American **Crafts**
Publishing, Inc
"The Creative Experience"

The Passionate
Beader's Guide
Best Techniques, Tools & Projects for Beading Success

President: **Jerry Cohen**

Chief Executive Officer: **Darren Cohen**

Editor: **Pamela Hawkins**

Assistant Editor: **Joanna Feller**

Editorial Assistant: **Jenni Simpson-Ackerman**

Art Director: **Kelly Albertson**

Graphic Designer: **Rory Wexler**

Technical Illustrator: **George Ahlers**

Photography:

Meridian Photo, www.meridianphoto.com

Wesley Demarest, Midhurst Studios

Pamela Hawkins

Tina Mori, www.tinas-photography.com

Take-One Studios

Product Development Director: **Vivian Rothe**

Printed in USA

ISBN-13: 978-1-60140-619-4
ISBN-10: 1-60140-619-3

Every effort has been made to ensure that all the information in this book is accurate. However, due to differing conditions, tools, and individual skills, All American Crafts, Inc., cannot be responsible for any injuries, losses, and other damages that may result from the use of the information in this book.

Produced by

All American Crafts, Inc.
7 Waterloo Road
Stanhope, NJ 07874
www.allamericancrafts.com

Published by

the art of everyday living

Leisure Arts, Inc.
5701 Ranch Drive
Little Rock, AR 72223
www.leisurearts.com

Introduction

The Passionate Beader's Guide is the result of our passion for all things beads, our desire to provide fun and inspiring projects to fit every aspect of your life, and our to wish educate you about the essential tools and techniques that will help build the backbone of your beading skills.

You'll notice a sidebar along the first right-hand page of each project. This sidebar contains a list of all of the tools necessary to complete each project, a list of the techniques and skills you can expect to learn, and space for you to write your own notes. Yes, you have our permission to *write* in this book! It is only natural for ideas to pop into our heads when we are being creative. So, as you work through each project and different bead colors, components, or design elements come to mind, go ahead and jot them down! You'll also find several pages in the back of the book where you can make notes and sketch your own designs.

This is *your* book. Keep your own notes as you work through it, bring it with you to your favorite bead store or beading class, and use it as a reference guide for all of your future beading adventures. It is our hope that this book will become as easy to use and as comfortable a companion as your favorite pair of round nose pliers!

Happy Beading!

Pamela

Pamela Hawkins
Editor

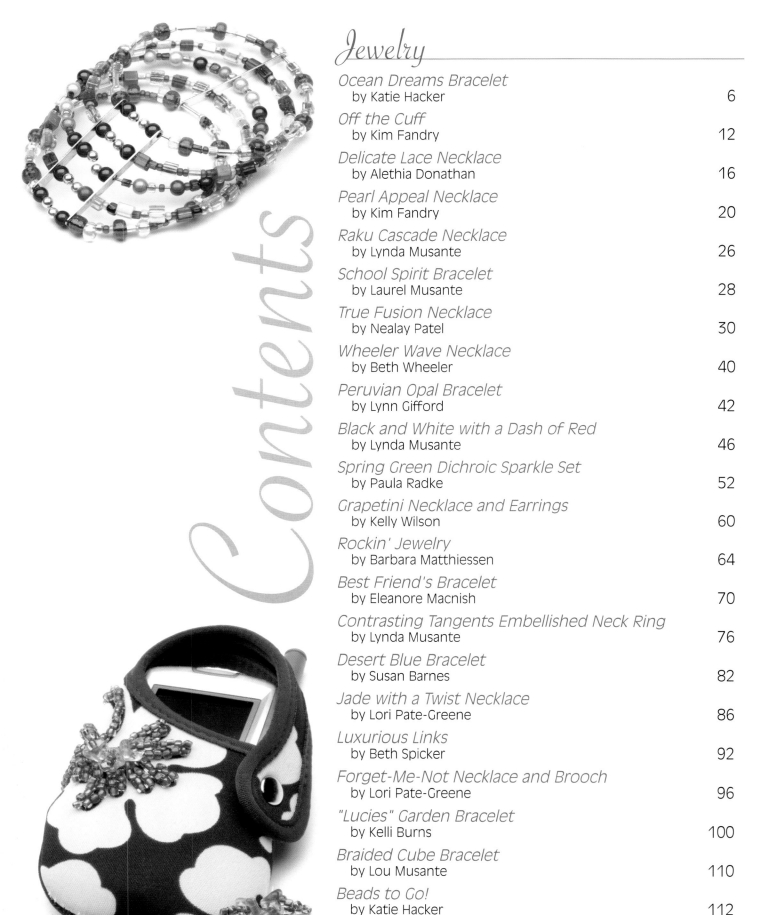

Jewelry

Contents

Home Décor

Fashion

Ocean Dreams Bracelet

Designed by Katie Hacker for Beadalon

Create this sparkling, multi-strand bracelet using simple stringing and crimping techniques. The elegant, fire-polished beads in blues and greens were inspired by the ocean waters, while the exposed flexible gold beading wire gives a fluid, wavelike feel.

Tips

• For a beginner version of this bracelet, create six beaded strands instead of 12 and attach two strands to each loop on the end piece. Use chain nose pliers to flatten the crimp beads instead of using a crimping tool to fold them.

• When making a multi-strand piece of jewelry, it can be difficult to keep all the components in the right places to see how well your bead and wire placements look visually. To make this easier, use a piece of foam core or cardboard as a work surface. Tape down all the cut strands on one side after crimping and after the bead tips have been added. This will make it easier to place beads and crimps throughout the wires and keep components properly spaced apart.

Dimensions

Approximately 7½ inches long

Materials

- 72 inches of flexible beading wire, .018-inch diameter—gold
- 98 assorted fire-polished glass beads, 5mm to 8mm—shades of blue, turquoise, teal
- 106 crimp beads, 1.3mm—gold
- 12 crimp beads, 1.5mm—gold
- 12 double-cup bead tips—gold
- 2 three-hole end pieces—gold
- Lobster clasp and jump ring—gold

Additional Supplies

Basic beading supplies, tape

For product information, see page 124.

Instructions

1. Cut twelve 6-inch lengths of beading wire using the wire cutters. Hold two strands together and string a 1.5mm crimp bead onto the end. Use crimping pliers to crimp it. String a bead tip onto the strands. Push it up to the crimp bead and use chain nose pliers to close the bead tip cups around the crimp bead (**Fig. 1**). Repeat this step to make six sets of two strands each. Attach two sets to each loop in one end piece, closing the bead tip loops with chain nose pliers (**Fig. 2**). *Note:* For easy assembly, use tape to secure end of bracelet to work surface while constructing strands.

2. String a 1.3mm crimp bead ½ inch from a bead tip on one strand. Crimp it. String one to three beads and another crimp bead to create one beaded section (**Fig. 3**). Crimp the crimp bead. String five beaded sections 1 inch apart. Each beaded section can consist of one to three beads.

3. On the other strand in the same set, string a 1.3mm crimp bead 1 inch from the bead tip. Crimp it. String one to three beads and another crimp bead to create a beaded section. Crimp the crimp bead. String four beaded sections 1 inch apart. Hold the strand ends together and string a bead tip and a 1.5mm crimp bead. Crimp the crimp bead and close the bead tip.

4. Repeat steps 2 and 3 to string beads onto all 12 strands.

5. Attach the opposite end of each of the beaded strand set to the corresponding loop on the other end piece. Use a jump ring to attach the lobster clasp to the outer ring on one of the end pieces (see Technique Guide, page 114).

Tools:

Chain nose pliers

Crimping pliers

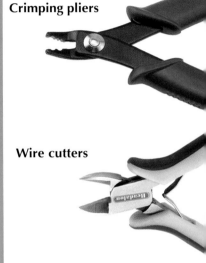

Wire cutters

Ruler

Techniques and Skills Learned:

- Stringing
- Crimping
- Multi-strand composition

Notes

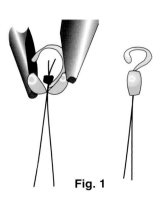

Fig. 1

Fig. 2

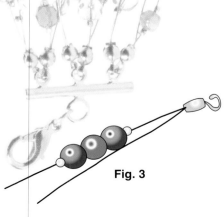

Fig. 3

Bead Adorned Knobs and Handles

Designed by Barbara Matthiessen

Use simple wire wrapping techniques to adorn common household hardware with sumptuous beads!

Tips

- Most hardware can be removed easily by unscrewing it from the back or inside of the piece.
- To use existing screw holes, measure the distance between the holes before making your beaded handles.
- To fill in screw holes and use your own bead-designed hardware, fill the holes with wood filler, allow to dry, sand smooth, and then apply paint or varnish to match finish.
- Drill new holes to match your hardware.
- Cruise through a hardware store with beading on your mind and see what other unique hardware parts are crying out to be beaded.

Dimensions

Various, depending on size of handle or knob

Note: All materials are listed *per knob.*

Flower Knob Materials

- 26-gauge beading wire—non-tarnish silver or copper
- 1½-inch eye screw
- Medium beads value pack—aqua

Additional Supplies

Basic beading supplies, drill (optional), screws to fit new hardware, wire, or chain

For product information, see page 124.

General Instructions

1. Choose wire that will easily fit through beads and chain links if using a chain. Cut wire cleanly from spool using wire cutters.

2. Secure wire to hardware by wrapping two or three times around and then folding back the wire's short end. Wrap two more times, or use round nose pliers to form a loop for inserting the screw later. Wrap wire around itself below loop at least two times (see Technique Guide, page 114).

3. Secure wire in the same way when finished beading. Cut any excess wire and file to smooth, if needed.

Flower Knob Instructions

1. Cut 12 inches of 26-gauge wire. Twist wire to secure it to base of eye screw (above screw threads).

2. Wrap wire twice around eye portion of hardware. To make first petal, string 1¼ inches of small aqua beads onto wire. Carefully fold beaded wire in half, and then wrap wire around eye. Repeat seven more times.

3. String two small aqua beads onto wire, and then wrap around eye in between petal wrappings. Repeat seven more times.

4. String largest aqua bead in the package on wire. Position bead in center of eye, then wrap both wire ends around eye and twist to secure.

5. Attach by drilling a hole to accommodate eye screw base and then threading on the nut.

Green Knob Materials

- 26-gauge beading wire—non-tarnish silver or copper
- 1½-inch eye screw—silver-tone
- Bead mix—green

Amber Knob Materials

- 26-gauge beading wire—non-tarnish silver or copper
- Disk spacers—copper
- 1½-inch lamp finial—brass
- Bead mix—amber

Instructions for Green or Amber Knobs

1. Cut a 20-inch piece of 26-gauge wire and secure it to the base of the eye screw or finial.

2. String a few mixed beads onto the wire. Wrap wire around the eye portion of the hardware. String on more mixed beads and wrap. Repeat, adding additional wire as needed to make a full ball of beads and securing wire to the eye each time.

3. Secure wire as in the general instructions.

4. Attach by drilling a hole to accommodate the eye screw base and then threading on the nut.

Tools:

Round nose pliers

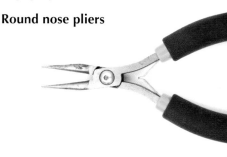

Wire cutters

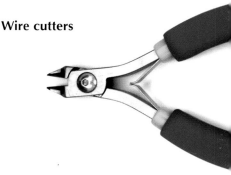

Ruler

Techniques and Skills Learned:

- Wirework:
  Embellished wire wrapping.

Notes

Amethyst Pull Materials
• 20-gauge beading wire—non-tarnish silver or copper
• 1 package assorted medium beads—amethyst
• 2 foiled oval beads—purple

Aqua/Silver Pull Materials
• 20-gauge beading wire—non-tarnish silver or copper
• 5 assorted medium beads—aqua
• 4 assorted medium spacers—imitation silver patina

Instructions for Amethyst and Aqua/Silver Wire Pulls
1. Cut a piece of 20-gauge wire to desired length (aqua/silver: 6½ inches; amethyst: 7½ inches; see Tips section). You will want some slack/drop on this piece to make it easily useable.

2. Follow general instructions for making a wrapped loop on one end.

3. String beads using photograph as a guide.

4. Complete by forming second wire loop.

5. Attach to drawer by inserting screw through wire loops on ends.

LOVE Handle Materials
• 26-gauge beading wire—non-tarnish silver or copper
• Disk spacers—hematite
• Typewriter key beads to spell "LOVE"
• 3-inch drawer handle

Turquoise Handle Materials
• 26-gauge beading wire—non-tarnish silver or copper
• Bead mix—turquoise/blue/silver
• 3-inch drawer handle

Instructions for Turquoise and LOVE Handles
1. Secure a length of 26-gauge wire to handle by wrapping around one end. *Note:* A 16-inch piece was used on the LOVE handle and two 20-inch pieces on the turquoise handle.

2. String a variety of turquoise/blue/silver beads on the handle, wrapping wire around the handle after every few beads. Add additional wire and beads for a full, varied look.

3. String four hematite disks on the LOVE handle and then wrap the wire around handle. Add "L" bead, wrap around handle. String eight hematite beads and wrap. Add "O" bead and wrap. Continue adding eight hematite beads and then one letter bead.

4. String four hematite beads after the "E" and then secure wire to handle. Attach by screwing through ends of handles.

Heart Pendant Pull Materials
• 26-gauge beading wire—non-tarnish silver or copper
• 4½-inch safety chain—silver-tone
• Glass heart pendant
• Bicone glass beads—blue sky

Instructions for Heart Pendant Pull
1. Cut chain to desired length. Remember to allow a full link for screw attachment.

2. Secure 12 to 15 inches of 26-gauge wire to one end of chain.

3. Weave wire through links, adding beads. Adjust the number and size of beads to size of chain links. Do not pull wire too tight or add so many beads that the chain will not flex, or both the wire and beads can break.

4. On the heart chain pull, add three layers of blue bicones by threading first through the center of links, placing the heart in the center, and then doing an overhand stitch at the top and bottom of the links.

5. When you've finished beading, secure wire to opposite end of chain.

6. Attach by screwing through end links.

Flower Knob

Aqua/Silver Pull

"Love" Handle

Amethyst Pull

Heart Pendant Pull

Green Knob

Amber Knob

Turquoise Handle

Off the Cuff Bracelet

Designed by Kim Fandry for The Bead Fetish

The combination of pounded metal, sparkling crystals, sliders, and freshwater pearls create a captivating bracelet. Master some basic wire working techniques while you construct this versatile design.

Tip

The beads on the materials list are simply a guideline. You may want to add more to the list or you may have a few leftovers for use in future projects. What's important is that you experiment and have fun doing it!

Dimensions

Approximately 7 inches

Materials

- 18 inches of 16-gauge dead soft wire—sterling silver
- 3 feet of 24-gauge dead soft wire—sterling silver
- 3 two-hole floral sliders
- 40 to 50 round beads, 2mm—sterling silver
- 24 to 30 Bali spacers, 4mm—sterling silver
- 2 to 3 oval Austrian crystals, 6mm x 9mm
- 9 to 12 Austrian crystal bicones, 6mm
- 4 rice freshwater pearls, 9mm
- 3 to 4 round freshwater pearls, 6mm
- 8 to 10 freshwater pearls, 5mm—rust or brown
- 2 to 4 Austrian crystal donuts, 6mm

Additional Supplies

Basic beading supplies

For product information, see page 124.

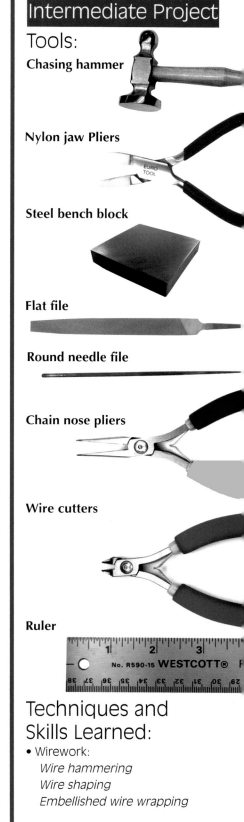

Intermediate Project

Tools:

Chasing hammer

Nylon jaw Pliers

Steel bench block

Flat file

Round needle file

Chain nose pliers

Wire cutters

Ruler

Techniques and Skills Learned:

- Wirework:
  Wire hammering
  Wire shaping
  Embellished wire wrapping

Notes

Instructions
Making the bracelet

1. Cut one 18-inch piece of 16-gauge wire. Straighten the wire with nylon jaw pliers.

2. Bend the wire in half, making a rounded curve—not a sharp bend. The two wire pieces should be spaced approximately 1 to 1½ inches apart (**Fig 1**). *Note:* Once you bend the wire, the ends will overlap. Straighten the wire again.

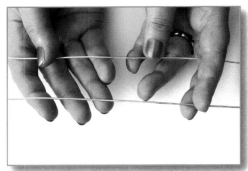

Fig. 1

3. Using the round needle file, file the holes in each floral slider until they fit onto the wire easily (**Fig. 2**). This shouldn't take long; a few twists of the file in each hole usually does the trick.

Fig. 2

4. Position the first slider on the two wire pieces about 1½ inches from the curved end. Add the next two sliders, each 1 inch apart (**Fig. 3**).

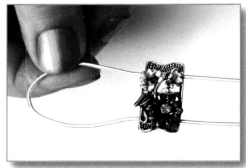

Fig. 3

5. Carefully make curved bends in the wires between the sliders by inserting the nylon jaw pliers in between the wire and slowly opening the jaws of the pliers (**Fig. 4**). Be careful not to open the jaws too fast or too far or else the side of the slider will break.

Fig. 4

6. Coil the ends of the wire into large spirals (**Fig. 5**). Start the spiral with the nylon jaw pliers, being careful not to square off the first bend. The wire is pretty soft, so once the spiral is started, you should be able to bend it with your fingers.

Fig. 5

7. Measure your wrist and the length of the bracelet, and adjust the spirals as needed. *Note:* To shorten the bracelet, tighten the spirals (which will use more wire). To lengthen the bracelet, unwind the spiral a little (to use less wire).

8. Using the bench block, begin hammering on the back of the bracelet. The wire will naturally begin to curl a bit as you hammer. Hammer on the corner of the block when flattening in between the sliders (**Fig. 6**). Continue hammering until all the wire has been slightly flattened. *Note:* Do not hit the sliders when hammering.

Fig. 6

9. Bind the spiral pairs on each end together with a small piece of 24-gauge wire. Wrap it around five or six times and cut off any excess at the back of the bracelet (**Fig. 7**). It's ok if the spirals overlap as you bind them together.

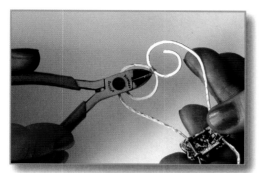

Fig. 7

10. Shape the bracelet by gently bending the wire (**Fig. 8**). As you bend, try it on for size and adjust to fit.

Fig. 8

Adding the beads

1. Cut a 2-foot piece of 24-gauge wire. Wrap the wire tightly around the curved end of the bracelet base several times to attach it. Trim the excess wire "tail" and file if necessary.

2. String about ¾ inch of beads on the wire, starting with a 2mm sterling silver bead, and then add a pearl, a crystal, and a sterling silver Bali spacer.

3. Attach the beaded wire at an angle to the other wire by pulling it slightly taut and wrapping it around the 16-gauge wire two times (**Figs. 9a and 9b**). Repeat three or four times within the space before the first slider.

Fig. 9a

Fig. 9b

4. Repeat steps 2 and 3 using various beads in the spaces between the sliders and after the third slider. Continue adding beads to the desired fullness.

5. Finish by wrapping the end of the 24-gauge wire tightly around the 16-gauge wire base several times. Cut off the excess wire at the back of the bracelet and file the end if necessary.

Delicate Lace Necklace

Designed by Alethia Donathan

Vintage bead-netted collars are intricate, gorgeous, and easy to wear. Try creating your own version with a creative and dimensional netted collar technique that uses seed beads and artist and pressed-glass beads.

Dimensions
16 inches long

Materials
- 2 tubes size 11/0 seed beads—blue
- 1 tube size 11/0 seed beads—raspberry
- 2 bead tips
- Gemstone chips or flower beads (optional)
- Clasp of choice

Additional Supplies
Basic beading supplies, crystal cement or clear nail polish

For product information, see page 124.

Instructions
Making the base

1. With a 3-foot piece of FireLine, string 16 blue seed beads, leaving an 8-inch tail. Pass back through bead #7 (**Fig 1**).

2. Add five seed beads and pass back through bead #1 (**Fig. 2**). Tie a

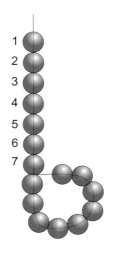

Fig. 1

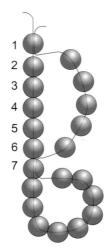

Fig. 2

Tools:

Beading needle and FireLine

Chain nose pliers

Beading scissors

Techniques and Skills Learned:
- Bead weaving:
  Netting
  Branch fringe
  Loop fringe
  Loop embellishment

Notes

knot with the tail and thread, but do not cut the tail.

3. Add five seeds and pass back through bead #3 of the first loop (**Fig. 3**).

4. Add five seeds and pass back through the third bead of the second loop (**Fig. 4**).

5. Add six seeds and pass back through the third bead of the second loop (**Fig. 5**).

6. Add five seeds and pass through the third bead of the first loop. (**Fig. 6**).

7. Repeat steps 3 through 6 until desired length is strung.

8. At 7 inches from the end, secure FireLine through several beads. Add 10 loop sections to base for two rows. Decrease by two loops and add two more rows, and again decrease by two loops

and add two more rows (the last row is only two loops). To increase, add 11 seeds (instead of six) at step 5 and pass back through the third bead in this set to form a loop. Continue through step 6. To decrease, repeat steps 5 and 6 as originally directed. *Note:* In the necklace pictured, the center section made with the increase is 1½ inches wide. The shorter base section is ½ inch wide on each side of the center.

9. To create height and dimension on the necklace base, add vertical loops (see Adding Loops inset photo). String a 2-foot piece of FireLine, secure the end in the base beads, and pass throug at a cross point (A) in the lace (**Fig. 7**). String seven seeds and pass back through the cross point bead A to form a loop. Work your way through the lace to the next

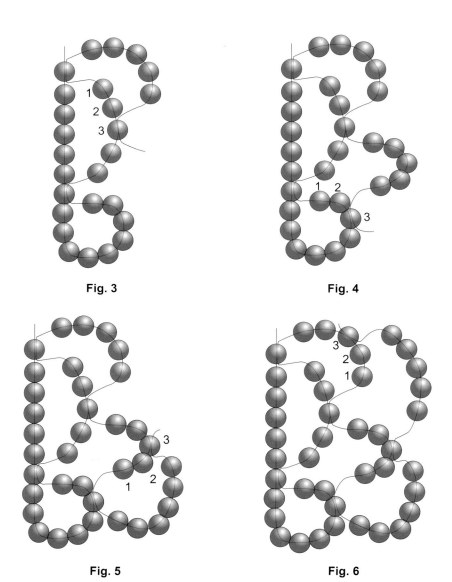

Fig. 3

Fig. 4

Fig. 5

Fig. 6

cross point and repeat for the entire piece, including the center extended section.

10. To create some variety in the loops, add chips or flower beads (**Fig. 8**). To add chips, make a loop by stringing three seeds, one chip, and three seeds. To add glass flowers, make a loop by stringing a flower bead, three seeds, and passing back through the flower bead. *Note:* Work raspberry seeds into these loops for color interest as well.

11. To finish, tie a knot at the top of the last row. Do not cut FireLine. Secure with crystal cement or clear nail polish. String a bead tip and tie a knot between the two shells. Secure with cement or polish and cut excess FireLine. With chain nose pliers, close until the two shells meet.

12. Attach clasp to the hook of the bead tip and close hook. Repeat for the opposite end.

Branch fringe

1. Anchor a 2-foot piece of FireLine and start from a cross point bead in the middle of the extended portion of the necklace.

2. String 20 blue seed beads, skip the first seed and pass back through four seeds. Add five seeds, skip the top seed, and pass back through four seeds into the original base row. Pass through two seeds on the base row (**Fig. 9**). Repeat to the top of the fringe.

3. If desired, use raspberry seeds to add berries to the fringe. String four raspberry seeds at the end of a branch and pass back through the first raspberry seed before passing back through the branch.

4. Make as many fringe pieces as desired, varying the length and number of branches as desired (see Fringe inset photo).

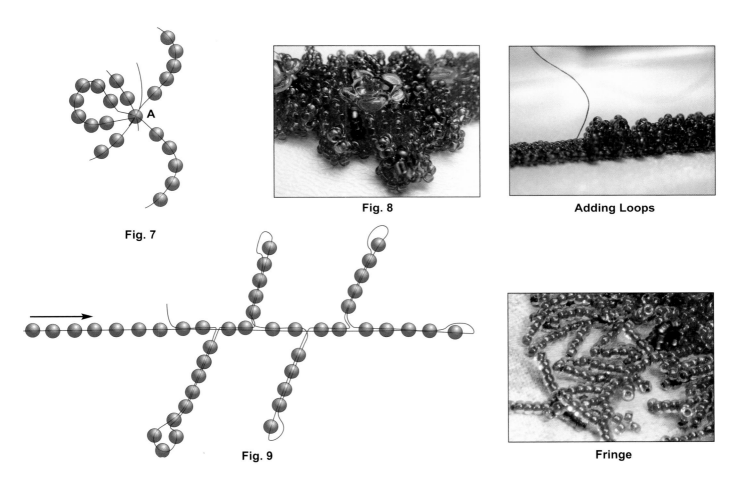

Fig. 7

Fig. 8

Adding Loops

Fig. 9

Fringe

Pearl Appeal Necklace

Designed by Kim Fandry for The Bead Fetish

Ribbon finish

This necklace is dazzling in a vintage yet very modern way.
A few wraps of cording and wire, strung with soft and delicate
pearls, create this stunning piece.

Color Palette

The sliders are available in 10 awesome colors, including topaz, emerald, and sapphire. All of the colors lend themselves beautifully to this project.

Tip

The design basis for this project is the balanced clustering of beads and sliders. I found that drawing the cones together in the back helped me keep the center in view, and I could make sure I was placing the beads and pearls evenly on both sides. Try this method and I think you'll be pleased with the end result.

Dimensions

Makes an adjustable-length necklace

Materials

- 5 two-hole sliders—fuchsia
- 100 to 150 metal beads, 2mm
- 18 to 20 rice-shaped freshwater pearls, 6mm
- 1 strand freshwater pearls, 4mm
- 2 to 5 freshwater pearl shapes (flat, round, etc.)
- 1 yard of 1mm woven cord or leather
- 4 to 6 feet of 28-gauge wire—silver
- 1 foot of 20-gauge wire—silver
- 2 cones—silver
- 4 feet of ribbon or silk cord (for alternate chain closure: 8 inches of chain, four 6mm freshwater pearls, four 1½-inch-long head pins that fit through the pearls, and one clasp of choice)

Additional Supplies

Basic beading supplies, velvet bead board or project board, straight pin, T-pin, or other type of pin

For product information, see page 124.

Chain finish

Tools:

Chain nose pliers

Round nose pliers

Flush cutters

Ruler

Beading scissors

Techniques and Skills Learned:

- Wirework:
  Wire wrapping
  Embellished wire wrapping
- Multimedia braiding

Notes

Instructions

Making the necklace base

1. Cut the piece of woven cord into three 1-inch pieces. Evenly gather the three ends, along with the end of the piece of 20-gauge wire. Grip all pieces firmly together in the base of the chain nose pliers (**Fig. 1**).

Fig. 1

2. Wrap the wire around the ends of the cord bundle as tightly as possible (**Fig. 2**). Bind the bundle together as one piece.

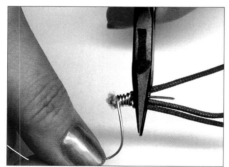

Fig. 2

3. Cut the short tail of the wire down to ¼ inch and fold it over the coil. Add the cone to the wire and place it over the wire coil (**Fig. 3**).

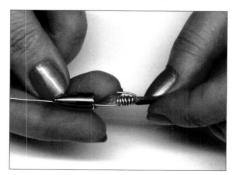

Fig. 3

4. Make a wire-wrapped loop at the end of the cone (**Fig. 4**).

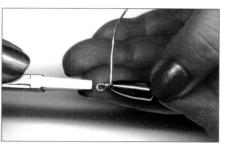

Fig. 4

5. Pin the wrapped loop to the project board and braid the woven cord or leather all the way to the ends (**Fig. 5**). *Note:* Don't make a braid that's so tight that the wire can't be threaded in and out. Repeat step 2 on this second end (**Fig. 6**).

Fig. 5

Fig. 6

Adding the sliders and beads

1. Cut a 2-foot length of 28-gauge wire and push one end into the cone (**Fig. 7**).

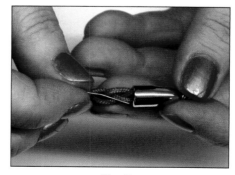

Fig. 7

2. Begin threading the wire in and out through the braid several times (**Fig. 8**). *Note:* Do not kink the wire as you work. Kinks create weak spots that can break easily if pulled too tight.

Fig. 8

3. Begin adding beads by first stringing one 2mm metal bead, one small freshwater pearl, and a second metal bead (**Fig. 9**). Attach by threading down through the braid, then coming back up in a different space. *Note:* I achieved the specific look of this necklace by adding 2mm metal beads on both sides of every freshwater pearl. Occasionally I would even add two or three metal beads in a row, either to fill a space or for a design element.

Fig. 9

4. When traveling across the braid to begin the next cluster of beads, thread the wire in and out of the braid, even going back and forth if you'd like. I intentionally made the wire obvious in between beaded clusters as part of the design. If you don't want to see the wire, simply thread the wire underneath one piece of cord and follow the braid on the back.

5. Select a position for the first two-hole slider (**Fig. 10**). Secure the slider firmly by passing wire through all four holes on the back. You don't need to do this all at once, but make sure they're each wired down before you move on.

Fig. 10

6. To add another length of wire, cut the existing wire to about 2 inches on the back of the necklace. Begin twisting a new 2½-foot piece of 28-gauge wire together with the 2-inch piece as close as possible to the point where the existing wire exits the back of the necklace (**Fig. 11**). Make about a ½-inch twist (a little shorter is fine). Trim the two short tails with the flush cutters.

Fig. 11

7. Continue working around the braid, adding beads, pearls, and sliders as desired using the same techniques described in steps 4 through 6. Use the necklaces in the photos for placement ideas.

8. Once you've reached the end of the necklace, thread the wire in and out and around the braid several times. Trim the wire end to measure 1 inch and push it into the cone with chain nose pliers.

Finishing the necklace

1. To finish with a ribbon or silk cord, cut the 4-foot piece in half. Thread one piece through the loop at the end of a cone and center it. Make an overhand knot and tighten it down around the wire loop. Tie the two ends together in a knot. Repeat this on the other side of the necklace. To wear it, simply tie a bow in the back.

2. To finish with a chain, stack each freshwater pearl on a head pin. Make a loop on both ends of three pins (see Technique Guide, page 114). Leave the "head" on one pearl as a stopper and make only one loop. Cut a 3-inch piece off the chain. Attach the 3-inch piece of chain to one side of the necklace using a double-looped pearl. To do this, open a loop on one side of the pearl, attach it to the end link of the chain, and then close the loop. Next, open the second loop on the pearl, attach it to the wire-wrapped loop on the end of one cone, and then close the loop. At the end of that same piece of chain, attach the clasp by using the same technique described earlier. Attach the remaining chain to the other side of the necklace in the same manner and add the pearl with the single loop to the end of that piece.

Jar Jewelry

Designed by Lori Pate-Greene
for The Beadery

If you think about it, a jar or vase has a neckline just as we do, so it only makes sense to dress it up. Learn how a few simple twists of wire can help you achieve any look.

Tips
• When twisting 28-gauge wire, do not twist it too much. Just twist enough to hold the bead in place.
• For a soft, more romantic look, use more than one color ribbon and make more than one bow.

Dimensions
Vary

Materials
• 2 packages assorted medium beads—amethyst
• 1 package assorted spacer beads—amethyst
• 1 package glass leaf and heart pendants—green
• 1 package 24-gauge wire—gold-tone
• 1 package 28-gauge wire—gold-tone
• Glass votive or pedestal candleholder
• 2 spools of ⁵⁄₁₆-inch-wide or ⅝-inch-wide ribbon—complementary colors

Additional Supplies
Basic beading supplies, pencil

For product information, see page 124.

Instructions
Note: Before beginning, check that the leaf and heart pendants have uniform loops. Use the round nose pliers to close each loop tightly.

1. Measure the circumference of the indented neck of the votive and add 5 inches to the measurement. Cut one piece of 24-gauge wire to that length.

2. Wrap one wire end around a pencil and twist to make a loop (**Fig. 1**).

3. String an assortment of beads and leaf and heart pendants, leaving ¹⁄₁₆ inch to ⅛ inch between

each bead and pendant (**Fig. 2**). *Note:* As you work, check the length of the wire around the votive neck. String only enough beads to fit around the neck.

4. When enough beads have been added to complete the votive "necklace," repeat step 2 to make a second loop. Trim any excess wire.

5. Cut a 24-inch piece of 28-gauge wire, and wrap one end in between two beads to anchor it to the necklace. Twist the short end of the wire to the long end to secure (**Fig. 3**).

6. String assorted medium beads and assorted spacer beads, leaving ½ inch to 1¾ inches of slack between beads (**Fig. 4a**). Twist beads to stabilize (**Figs. 4b** and **4c**). String a few beads at different lengths between each bead in the base row (**Fig. 5**).

7. Place the beaded "necklace" around the votive neck. Thread a 16-inch piece of ribbon through both wire loops and tie a bow to finish (**Fig. 6**).

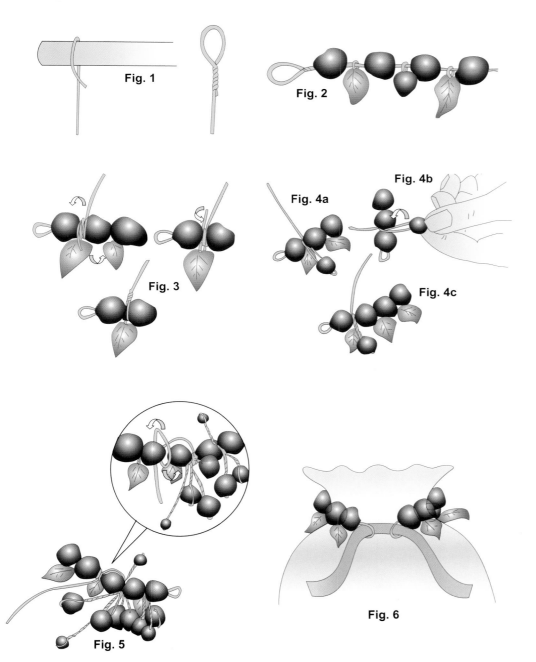

Fig. 1

Fig. 2

Fig. 3

Fig. 4a

Fig. 4b

Fig. 4c

Fig. 5

Fig. 6

Tools:

Round nose pliers

Wire cutters

Ruler

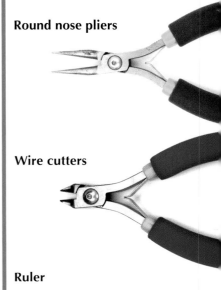

No. R590-15 **WESTCOTT**

Techniques and Skills Learned:

- Wirework:
  Embellished wire wrapping

Notes

Raku Cascade Necklace

Designed by Lynda Musante

Stringing, crimping, and some basic wirework come together to combine the rich, unpredictable colors of Raku beads with artisan fibers and colored metal stringing wire into a one-of-a-kind necklace.

Tip

If any of your Raku beads are chipped, touch up the edges by lightly brushing the chipped edge against the surface of the dye inkpad. This will camouflage the chip.

Dimensions

22 inches long

Materials

- 60 feet of .019 beading wire—steel
- 30 feet of .019 beading wire—golden bronze
- 2 Bali cones—silver
- Bali "S" clasp—silver
- 2 large Raku focal beads
- 11 round Raku beads, 9mm
- 9 flat, square Raku beads, 10mm
- 7 flat, round Raku beads, 8mm
- 30 crimp tubes, 2mm—sterling silver
- 2 crimp tubes, 3mm—sterling silver
- 2 artisan yarns—to coordinate with Raku beads
- 16 feet of half-hard wire—sterling silver
- Jump ring, 4mm—silver

Additional Supplies

Basic beading supplies, beading board with three rows, tea stain-colored dye inkpad

For product information, see page 124.

Instructions

1. Begin arranging the Raku beads on the beading board, positioning the two large focal beads about 3½ inches to the left and right of the center point. Reserve two round Raku beads for finishing the necklace.

2. Arrange the smaller beads randomly, using three rows on the beading board and creating an arrangement of beads that covers 20 inches.

3. Cut a 30-inch length of steel-colored beading wire. Pass through the middle bead in the first row and center it on the wire. Pass through a 2mm crimp tube, and then pass through the next bead to the left. Place this bead back onto the beading board. Slide the crimp up to the base of the bead and crimp it. Add another crimp tube and pass through the next Raku bead in the same bead row. Continue stringing and strategically crimping until you reach the focal bead. String the wire through the focal bead and continue the pattern until you reach the end of that row.

4. Repeat step 3 with the next two rows of beads on the left side, using the bronze-colored wire for one row and the steel-colored wire for the last row. Each wire should pass through the large focal bead.

5. String the right side of all three wires, again making sure that each wire passes through the large focal bead.

6. Gather the three strands of wire on each side and pass the strands through one 3mm crimp tube. Hold up necklace to see how the strands look. You want to position the strands so they drape nicely, one below the next (refer to photo). When satisfied with the arrangement, crimp the 3mm crimp tubes on each side.

7. Cut three or four lengths of artisan yarn. Weave each strand in and out among the beads. When finished, lift and drape the necklace again to check how the yarn looks with the beads. Make any adjustments you wish.

8. Cut an 8-inch length of half-hard wire and file each end. Using the round nose pliers, start a loop in the center of the wire, but do not close it. Place the wire about 1 inch from the last bead on the necklace, and then fold the yarn and wire over the wire loop (**Fig. 1**).

9. Close the loop and use one leg of the wire to tightly wrap the folded yarn and wire to secure it (**Fig. 2**). Trim excess wire on the wrapped end.

10. Insert the remaining wire end through the bead cone and add one round Raku bead. Begin a wrapped loop. Add a jump ring before closing the loop. Close the loop and finish the wrapped loop.

11. Repeat steps 8 through 10 to complete the opposite end of the necklace.

Fig. 1

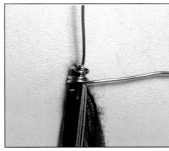

Fig. 2

Intermediate Project

Tools:

Chain nose pliers

Crimping pliers

Wire cutters

Wire file

Ruler

Techniques and Skills Learned:

- Stringing
- Crimping
- Wirework:
  Wire wrapping

Notes

Jewelry

School Spirit Bracelet

Designed by Laurel Musante

Spirit Squads 81

Learn how to manipulate memory wire as you make this bracelet to **match any sports team** or **school color scheme.**

Tips
- Create your own pattern and repeat it throughout the whole project.
- Use two pairs of pliers and bend the memory wire back and forth until it snaps. *Do not cut* the memory wire.

Materials
- 1 package of bracelet-sized memory wire—silver
- 10 memory wire end caps—silver
- 3 five-hole spacer bars—silver
- 1 package miracle beads, 3mm—pink/white/red mix*
- 1 package cube beads, 3mm—pink/white/red mix*
- 1 tube size 8/0 seed beads—pink/white/red mix*
- 1 tube bugle beads, 4mm—silver

*Select bead mixes in your team or school colors.

Additional Supplies
Basic beading supplies, cyanoacrylate glue

For product information, see page 124.

Instructions
1. Measure wrist and, using the technique described in the Tips section, break five individual rings of memory wire long enough to fit around your wrist.
2. Glue a memory wire end cap to one end of each memory wire ring. Let dry overnight.
3. After the glue has dried, add one miracle bead to the first wire coil. Pass through a five-hole spacer bar.
4. Continue adding beads in your chosen pattern.
5. When the wire is half full, add the second five-hole spacer.
6. Continue stringing beads. Add the last five-hole spacer about 2 cm from the wire end.
7. Add a miracle bead, glue on the memory wire end cap, and let dry.
8. Repeat steps 3 through 7, using the second wire coil and passing it through the second hole in each spacer bar.
9. Repeat steps 3 through 7 with remaining three wire coils, passing each through the correct holes in the spacers.

Tools:

Chain nose pliers (two pairs)

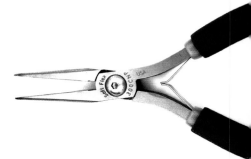

Techniques and Skills Learned:
- Stringing
  Multi-strand composition

Notes

True Fusion Necklace

Designed by Nealay Patel

Become a bead-weaving pro as you work the intricate stitches to complete this show-stopping, asymmetrical piece.

Dimensions
16 inches long

Materials
- 2 tubes of seed beads (one in each color)—blue and white
- 2 tubes of bugle beads (one in each color)—blue and clear
- 6 bicone crystals, 6mm—clear
- Clasp—sterling silver
- 9 jump rings—sterling silver
- 4 eye pins—sterling silver
- 24 inches of jewelry chain—sterling silver

Additional Supplies
Basic beading supplies

For product information, see page 124.

Tools:

Beading needle and nylon-coated beading thread

Beading scissors

Chain nose pliers

Round nose pliers

Wire cutters

Techniques and Skills Learned:
- Bead weaving
- Wirework:
  Wire wrapping

Notes

Instructions

Note: Construct the full wheels (steps 1 through 5) using clear bugles and blue seeds. Construct the semicircles (steps 6 through 12) using blue bugles and white seeds.

1. String a bugle, a seed, and a bugle and pass back through the first bugle to form a circle (**Fig. 1**).

2. String three seeds. Skip the last seed, pass back through the first two seeds and the bugle, add a seed, and then pass through the second bugle (**Fig. 2**).

3. Repeat steps 1 and 2 until 22 bugles are stitched. *Note:* The work will take on a curved shape. To close the circle, repeat step 1 using the first bugle instead of adding a new bugle. Repeat step 2 to add the final seed spike (top and bottom). Work the thread through the beads to secure and trim excess.

4. Create a total of four wheels—three using 22 bugles and one using 28 bugles.

5. Arrange the four wheels in a diamond shape, positioning the largest wheel at the top. Stitch the wheels together by passing through the top of the bead spikes (**Fig. 3**).

6. Repeat step 1.

7. Pass through seed #1 again, pick up three seeds, and pass back through seed #1 and bugle #2 (**Fig. 4**).

8. Pick up a seed and pass back through bugle #1, seed #1, and bugle #2. Add a bugle and a seed, pass through bugle #2, add a seed, and pass back through bugle #3 (**Fig. 5**).

9. Continue by stringing on a seed, a bugle, and a seed and passing through bugle #3.

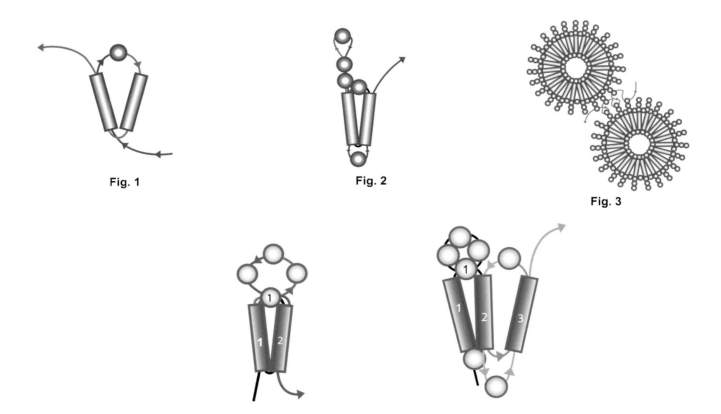

Fig. 1

Fig. 2

Fig. 3

Fig. 4

Fig. 5

10. Repeat steps 7-9 until 12 bugles are strung (**Fig. 6**). Pass thread through the bottom seeds to create a semicircle fan shape, called semicircle A.

11. Following steps 5-9, create a second semicircle, with 23 bugles (semicircle B). Set both semicircles aside.

12. Repeat step 1, pass back through the seed and bugle, add a seed, and pass back through the other bugle and top seed. Continue adding seeds and bugles until 25 bugles are strung, making semicircle C (**Fig. 7**). Make two more semicircles, one with 13 bugles (semicircle D) and one with six bugles (semicircle E). For each semicircle, pass thread through the bottom seeds as shown in **Fig. 6**.

13. Stitch semicircle A to the back of the beaded piece as shown in **Fig. 8**. The beaded unit may be reversed to make stitching easier. Starting at the top of the last bugle strung (indicated by red thread), pass through the seed between the spikes and then pass back through the end bugle. From there, sew into the second seed between the spikes. Pass through the bottom seeds of the semicircle to the other end. Pass through a seed between spikes and then pass through the end bugle. Finish by passing through the last seed, and then secure the thread in the beadwork. *Note:* Not all measurements are exact. Place the semicircle where sewing is easiest for you.

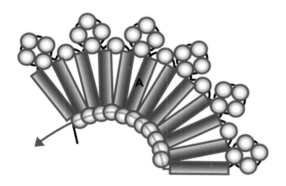

Fig. 6

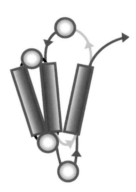

Fig. 7

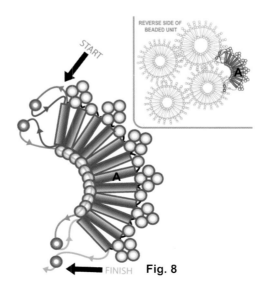

START

FINISH   **Fig. 8**

REVERSE SIDE OF
BEADED UNIT

A

14. Referring to **Fig. 9,** stitch semicircle E to the backside of the main piece.

15. Referring to **Fig. 10a** for overall placement and **Fig. 10b** for details, stitch semicircle C to the front side of the beaded piece.

16. Referring to **Fig. 11,** stitch semicircle B to the front side of the beaded piece, noting how it intertwines with semicircle C.

17. Referring to **Fig. 12,** stitch semicircle D to the beaded piece. Note that the bottom of the semicircle is stitched into the front of the piece and the top is stitched into the back of the piece. The completed beaded piece should look like **Fig. 13.**

18. Using the ladder stitch, connect 18 blue bugles (see Technique Guide, p. 114). Fold the ladder in half and pass it through the beaded piece, referring to **Fig. 14** for placement. Stitch the two ladder ends together to form a ladder loop. Starting with a new thread, pick up two blue bugles and pass through the top of the ladder loop and pass back through one of the new bugles.

19. Add a crystal, a blue bugle, and four white seeds. Pass through the bugle and four seeds again.

20. Pick up a blue bugle and a white seed, and pass through the last three seeds from step 18 plus

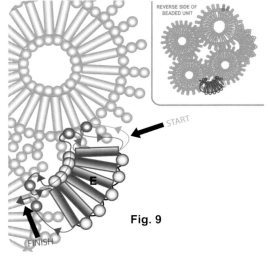

Fig. 9

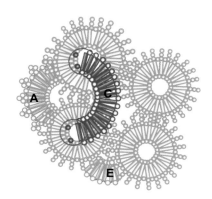

Fig. 10a

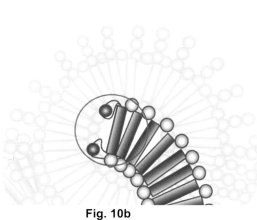

Fig. 10b

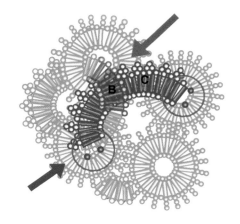

Fig. 11

the seed just strung (**Fig. 15**). Repeat this step to create the length of beaded spiral necklace desired.

21. To attach one side of the clasp, pass through the clasp's jump ring several times and then pass back through the beads in the beaded spiral.

22. Add a crystal to an eye pin and create a loop just above the crystal (see Technique Guide, p. 114). Repeat to make a total of four crystal eye pins.

23. Cut four lengths of chain: 5 inches, 5⅛ inches, 5¼ inches, and 6 inches. Attach a crystal eye pin from step 21 to one end of each chain using a jump ring. Again using jump rings, attach the opposite end of each crystal eye pin to the beaded piece, referring to the photo for placement ideas. *Note:* Attach the chains in such a way that the piece hangs nicely. Attach the opposite end of each chain onto one jump ring, and attach that jump ring to the second half of the clasp.

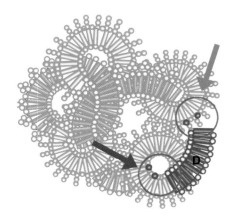

Fig. 12

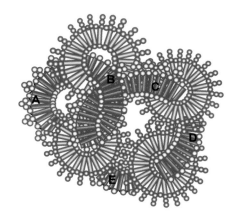

Fig. 13

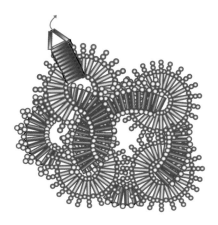

Fig. 14

Fig. 15

Home Décor

Copper Candlelight

Designed by Barbara Matthiessen

A little metalwork and some simple wire shaping allow you to create these warm and glowing accessories for your home.

Inspiration

Copper has long been my favorite metal. I adore the rich, weathered look of antiquity in patina copper and the warm, sunny feel of polished copper. Adding beads to copper is the frosting on the cake! Turquoise and copper are so attractive together, yet almost any color looks fabulous and bead finishes from matte to sparkling crystal complement this chameleon metal.

Tips

• Copper candleholders are hard to find. The one shown in this project is a tin candleholder painted to resemble tarnished copper.
• On the large candleholder, mix in leftover beads from other projects to add interest to the dangles.
• Add as many bead dangles to the large holder as desired—the more the merrier!
• When working with metals, be aware that cut edges can be sharp. Wear gloves to prevent nicks.
• ALWAYS use tongs and pot holders when heating metal, and allow it to cool completely before handling.

Dimensions

Small votive: 3 inches
Large candleholder: 8 inches
Wire mesh Bobèche: vary

Materials

Small votive
- 1 tube of soft, lightweight metal sheets with wood tool
- 1 spool of 22-gauge wire—copper
- 1 strand of turquoise chips

Large candleholder
- Sturdy metal candleholder of choice
- Spray paint—copper and matte black (for faux tarnished copper finish)
- 1 spool 18-gauge wire—copper
- 1 spool 22-gauge wire—copper
- Leaf-shaped beads of choice
- E beads of choice

Wire mesh Bobèche
Flat-top candleholder and candle of choice
Pliable wire metal mesh—copper
8 to 10 glass leaf beads—green
2 packages of foiled pressed beads—green
1 spool of 24-gauge wire—copper

Additional Supplies

Basic beading supplies, disappearing ink marker, heat-proof surface, pot holders, spray bottle filled with water (for faux tarnished copper finish)

For product information, see page 124.

Small Votive Instructions

1. To cut the copper sheet to measure 4½ inches x 11½ inches, place the ruler on the sheet and mark the appropriate line(s) with the wood tool. Cut along the marked line(s) with scissors, being careful of sharp edges.

2. Fold ¼-inch to ½-inch hems on both long sides of the copper. Fold metal up to the ruler edge, and then remove ruler and smooth the flat with the side of the wood tool (**Figs. 1 and 2**).

3. Heat tinge copper with propane/butane lighter or over the flames of a propane grill (**Fig. 3**). *Important:* Use tongs and pot holders during this process because the metal will get very hot. Wave the copper next to the flame and watch for color changes. *Note:* Do not overheat and burn through the copper. Place on heat-proof surface to cool completely before continuing.

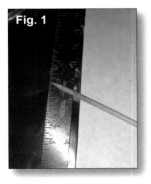
Fig. 1

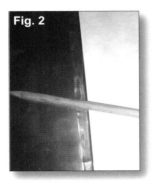
Fig. 2

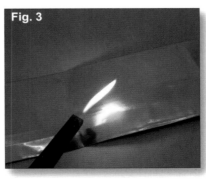
Fig. 3

Tools:

Propane-type lighting torch or propane grill

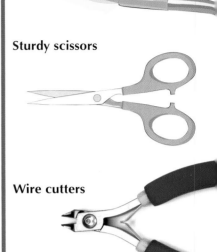

Sturdy scissors

Wire cutters

Ruler

Techniques and Skills Learned:
- Stringing
- Metalwork:
  Working with metal sheets
- Wirework:
  Embellished wire wrapping
  Creating wire spirals
  Wire shaping

Notes

4. To fold the cooled copper, place it wrong side down (seams up) on work surface. Following **Fig. 4**, measure and then make the following folds (all folded upwards): ½ inch, 1½ inches, 2½ inches, 2½ inches, 2½ inches, 1½ inches. Make another ½-inch fold downward using the remaining copper.

5. Slide the outer ½-inch folded ends together and then press to secure, creating a square copper votive.

6. Thread enough turquoise chips onto the wire to fit around the copper votive. Wrap beaded wire around the middle of the votive, pull tight so beaded wire fits snugly around the copper, and then twist the wire ends together on the side with the metal seam. Trim wire ends to 3 inches. Tuck wire ends under the folded seam at top and bottom.

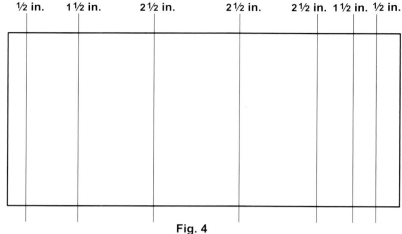

Fig. 4

Large Candleholder Instructions

1. If your candleholder does not have holes around the top, drill ⅟₃₂-inch diameter holes every ¼ inch to ½ inch around the top edge. File any rough edges as needed.

2. If your candleholder is not copper, spray paint it copper following the paint manufacturer's instructions for application and drying time. To age the copper finish, mist with water, and while wet, spray lightly with black paint. Quickly dab the surface using an unprinted plastic bag. Allow paints to cure.

3. Using approximately 36 inches of 22-gauge. wire, pass wire through the first and second hole, and twist wire together to secure. Bring wire to the outside. String on a few E beads and insert wire from outside to inside through the next hole. Add more E beads, and then pass wire back out to front through next drilled hole. String stones, ovals, or other beads of choice on wire to fit the spaces between drilled holes. Use E beads to cover wire as it passes through drilled holes and on the inside of the candleholder. Continue all the way around the top of the candleholder. If more wire is needed, cut another piece and secure the same way as for the first piece.

4. Cut a 10 inch piece of 18-gauge wire and twist a spiral at one end using round nose pliers. Add beads of choice, and then make a small loop at the top (see Technique Guide p.114). Open the loop and secure around the beaded wire made in step 3. Repeat, making a variety of shapes and sizes of dangles. Refer to photo for ideas. Bend and shape wires and vary the number and bead spacing to add interest.

Large Candleholder

Wire Mesh Bobèche

1. Place candle onto metal mesh and trace around it using the disappearing ink marker. Cut out the traced piece with sturdy scissors.

2. *Outer edge.* Bead the outer edge of the mesh by stringing foil beads on copper wire. Loop a piece of 24-gauge wire through the edge of the mesh, string on two foil beads, loop the wire around edge of mesh and then back through the mesh even with the end of the last bead.

3. *Dangle fringe.* To make leaf dangle fringe, secure wire end near the mesh edge and string three foil beads, a leaf bead, and one more foil bead on wire. Pass wire around last foil bead and back up through the leaf and remaining foil beads. Twist wire around top of fringe. To make short fringe, string on two foil beads, skip the last bead and pass wire through the next bead, wrap around the main wire, and then repeat to make a second two-bead strand. Wrap wire around main wire and then back up through the mesh. Weave wire through edge of mesh for about ⅛ inch, then create a second short fringe and bring wire back up through mesh edge (**Fig. 5**). Repeat fringe around entire piece, alternating between long fringe and short. Secure wire and trim excess.

Wire Mesh Bobèche Instructions

Bobèche is a French term that refers to a collar at the base of a candle used to catch wax drippings. These can be made from a variety of items such as crystal, glass, or paper. Sometimes, there are beaded dangles or drops that are also used for the same purpose.

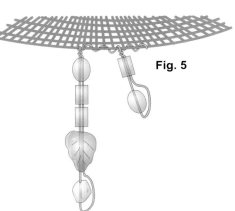

Fig. 5

Jewelry

Wheeler Wave Necklace

Designed by Beth Wheeler

Learn a technique for curling beading wire as you complete this flowing, three-strand necklace.

Inspiration

I wanted to do something creative with the wire.......and I love how ribbon curls and swirls on gift packages. I thought, "wouldn't it be neat if these wires did the same?" So, this necklace is the result of that creative exploration.

Tips

• Use clear-coated wire, not colored. The coating on colored wire is easily damaged by the friction used in the curling step.
• The curling step should NOT compromise the integrity of the coating on the wire.
• Choose small beads to minimize the weight of the necklace and to preserve as much curl as possible.
• This necklace is perfect for using up some of the "bead soup" mixes you have left over from other projects.

Dimensions

Vary based on tightness of curl

Materials

- 10 foot spool of .024 beading wire—clear
- 12 crimp beads, 3mm—silver
- 3 packages of small beads—color of choice
- Toggle clasp—silver

Additional Supplies

Basic beading supplies, cellophane tape

For product information, see page 124.

Instructions

1. First strand: Leaving wire on spool, string one package of small beads onto the end of the wire, alternating large and small beads to fill a length of wire approximately 25 inches long (don't cut wire from the spool). Remember that the curling will shorten the length of your necklace. Slide all the beads toward the spool, leaving a long tail equal to the length of beads on the wire, (25 inches) as in **Fig. 1**.

2. Keeping a 2-inch tail, wrap a piece of cellophane tape around the wire end to pre-vent beads from sliding. Curl the remaining 23-inch tail between your finger and thumbnail, or with the blunt edge of a pair of closed scissors like curling ribbon (**Fig. 2**). *Note:* Practice curling pieces of wire until you are comfortable with the pressure necessary to achieve the desired curl. The pressure on the wire will determine the tightness of the curl. The goal is to curl the wire as much as possible without damaging the coating on the wire. The curl will relax (a lot) when the weight of the beads is added, so plan more curl than you want in the finished necklace— about three times more curl!

Fig. 1

3. Begin working the beads through the curls to the end (**Fig. 3**). When all beads have been worked onto the curled wire and checked to eliminate any gaps between beads, leave a 2-inch tail and cut the wire from the spool. Secure the cut end with tape to prevent beads from sliding off.

Fig. 2

4. Repeat steps 1-3 with the wire and remaining beads to create a total of three strands. Add 1 inch to the second strand and 2 inches to the third strand.

5. For each wire end, pass the wire through two crimp beads, through the clasp end, and back through the two crimp beads. (This is a double crimp.) Snug up the wire to the clasp end, leave ½ inch to 1 inch of excess wire, and crimp both crimp beads (see Technique Guide, p. 114). Tuck excess wire into the first few beads on each strand.

Fig. 3

Tools:

Crimping pliers

Wire cutters

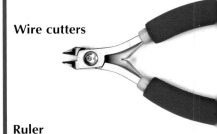

Ruler

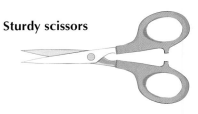

Sturdy scissors

Techniques and Skills Learned:

- Stringing
- Curling nylon-coated beading wire

Notes

Jewelry

Peruvian Opal Bracelet

Designed by Lynn Gifford

The Peruvian blue opal stones showcased in this wirework bracelet create an elegant look that goes beyond your average bead. Find out for yourself how versatile wire can be as you make this project.

Tips

• Use caution when working with wire; keep long pieces away from your face when working on the top of your piece. Always cover your hands over the piece you are cutting or hold both sides of the wire.

• Only rework wire two or three times—the wirework hardens with each movement and overworked wire can become brittle and break.

• When working with natural stones, gold-filled wire may be a better choice. Sterling silver will tarnish, and dipping a piece to clean it can damage natural stones.

Dimensions

7½ inches long

Materials

• 2 feet of 22-gauge square ½ gold-filled hard wire (exact amount varies depending on wrist size)

• 6 feet of 24-gauge round ½ gold-filled hard wire

• 16-inch strand of Peruvian opal beads or natural stones

• 6 Peruvian opal medium focal beads or coordinating beads of choice

• 6 gold-filled balls, 3mm

• 6 gold-filled balls, 4mm

Additional Supplies

Basic beading supplies, marker, masking tape

For product information, see page 124.

Note: The materials and instructions listed are for making a 7½-inch bracelet. For a larger or smaller bracelet, measure your wrist and add about 2 inches when cutting the base (square) wire.

Instructions

Building the base

1. Cut two 9½-inch lengths of 22-gauge square wire with the wire cutters. Tape the wires together with masking tape, leaving 2 inches of bare wire exposed at each end. When taping, make sure to keep the wires lying flat and side by side. Do not allow them to overlap.

Tools:

Chain nose pliers (2 pairs)

Flat nose pliers

Flush cutters

Round nose pliers

Ruler

Techniques and Skills Learned:

• Wirework:
   Wire wrapping
   Wire shaping
   Embellished wire
     wrapping

Notes

2. Use the round nose pliers to bend one wire only, making a loop 1 inch from the end (**Fig. 1**). Use flat nose pliers to pinch the ends tight, leaving the folded edge as a round loop (**Fig. 2**).

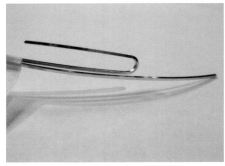

Fig. 1

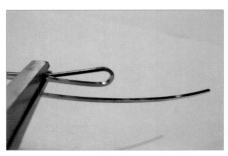

Fig. 2

3. To bind, hold all three wire pieces (two original plus the one folded down) together at the pinch mark with the flat nose pliers in your non-dominant hand. Grab the non-looped wire with the chain nose pliers and wind it tightly around the three wires (**Fig. 3**). Wrap toward the loop and trim the end with the flat side of your wire cutters (**Fig. 4**). Remember, always cover the piece you are cutting with your hands or hold both sides of the wire for protection from flying pieces. Tuck the small, sharp edge into the base with the chain nose pliers. Peel the tape off at this end.

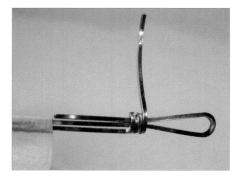

Fig. 3

Fig. 4

4. Using the chain nose pliers, bend the small tail remaining from the first wire back toward the loop, making a U-turn (**Fig. 5**). This keeps the wire from slipping out. Cut off the excess tail wire and flatten the cut edge with chain nose pliers. *Note:* Trim the tail on the top of the bracelet so you have smooth wire against your skin. The top will be covered with beads, so it won't show.

Fig. 5

5. Measure the bracelet to fit by forming the base into an oval shape. The ends should meet in the middle of the long side of the oval. When bracelet fits comfortably, make a mark where the wire crosses the curve of the loop to designate the location of the hook closure.

6. To make the smaller loop for the hook, grab one wire ½ inch from the mark toward the wire end with the round nose pliers. Use the pliers to create a small loop (**Fig. 6**).

Fig. 6

7. Pinch the entire small loop closed with the flat nose pliers so it will fit through the loop on the other end. Bind all three wires together to the outside of the mark following step 3 (**Fig. 7**).

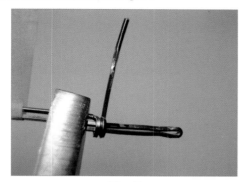

Fig. 7

8. Use the round nose pliers to grab the small loop and curve it away from the bracelet, making sure that the "hook" you create will hold firmly onto the loop to secure the bracelet (**Fig. 8**).

Fig. 8

Adding on the beads

1. Start at one end of the bracelet with 18 inches of 24-gauge round wire. Wrap it around the base two times and flatten with flat nose pliers. Cut off the remaining wire tail and tuck it into the base with chain nose pliers (**Fig. 9**).

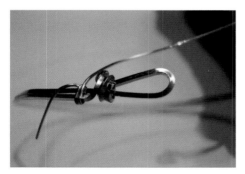

Fig. 9

2. Add a bead and wrap around the entire base one time. Add another bead and repeat.

3. Be sure to cover your binding at each end with beads (**Fig. 10**). Keep beads a safe distance from the hook.

Fig. 10

4. Work from one end of the bracelet to the other and then back again, if necessary (**Fig. 11**). Add in gold-filled balls as you go. If you are using focal beads, add them during your first pass. Bracelet may straighten out as you are working, so keep reshaping it into an oval as you add beads. Make sure to always position the beads on the top of the base; otherwise, the finished bracelet size will be smaller than planned and some beads will be hidden on the inside of your bracelet.

Fig. 11

5. Add wire in 18-inch sections as needed. Continue adding beads and securing to the base until you have your desired look. Add in fewer beads for a more delicate look. Add in more beads for a chunkier look. Want a fuller look with less visible wire? Add four or five beads at the same time and then wrap around the base twice.

Jewelry

Black and White with a Dash of Red

Designed by Lynda Musante

Two types of peyote stitch and a few improvisational variations in the beadwork will result in a splendid and visually dynamic necklace.

Classic Colors Create a Fun Design

Red, white, and black create a popular color and design combination, and these focal beads are really fun. Try a color palette in a similar fashion with other lampwork or large focal beads. Choose three colors that work best with the beads. Sprinkle a few seed bead colors at the base of your focal bead to get a visual look at how the colors complement each other. Remember that the focal bead should be the center of attention.

My challenge with this project was to combine the three basic colors in an interesting way that didn't distract from the patterns on the lampwork beads. My solution was to include a lot of open spaces by adding arches. Through the addition of arches and bridges, the feeling of movement was created. The base strip of beadwork was created and then the arches and bridges were looped and twisted around the base strip before they were attached. Each of the focal beads has seed beads strung through the hole for support and strength.

The sterling silver slide clasp has three rings on each side for attachment. This style of clasp is primarily used in stringing projects, but it worked well with the peyote-stitched beadwork, as it helps the beadwork to appear as a continuing band.

Tips

• Be sure your bugle beads have been culled to eliminate any that are broken or have sharp edges.
• For visual interest, I will often gently twist the necklace before wearing it.

Dimensions
19 inches long

Materials
• 1 tube size 11/0 Japanese seed beads—red
• 1 tube size 11/0 Japanese hex seed beads—black
• 1 tube size 11/0 Czech seed beads—cream
• 1 tube size 8/0 seed beads—red
• 1 tube short bugle beads—red
• 1 tube long bugle beads—black
• 3 large lampwork glass beads
• 2 smaller lampwork accent beads—to coordinate with large beads
• Silver slide clasp with 3 rings per side

Tools:

Size 12 beading needle and size B nylon beading thread

Beading scissors

Techniques and Skills Learned:
• Stringing
• Bead weaving:
  Basic peyote stitch
  Two-drop peyote stitch

Notes

Additional Supplies

Basic beading supplies, necklace design board

For product information, see page 124.

Stitch Techniques

Basic Peyote Stitch

See the Technique Guide on page 114 for information on basic peyote stitch.

Two Drop Peyote

In this variation, you add two beads at a time, but treat them as a set. You will stitch through both beads as if they are a single bead. They will be counted as a single bead as well. If you are planning a project that will combine beads of different sizes in a piece, consider using double peyote stitch so you have the choice of adding two smaller beads as a set in combination with a single larger bead. This technique works especially well if you are combining 11/0 beads and 8/0 beads.

1. Thread on a tension bead, and then add an even number of two-bead sets (12 beads). Bring the needle around and pass through the fifth and sixth beads (the two beads in the third set).

2. Continue adding two beads per set until you reach the end of the row.

3. Turn the piece and add two beads at a time to build up the rows. At the end of the third row, it should be easy to see the hills and valleys created by the peyote stitch. You will add the sets of beads in the valleys and stitch through the hills (**Fig. 1**).

Arches and Bridges:
Creating Open Spaces and Texture

1. To create a gap within the beadwork, begin to add arches. To create an arch, string on 1 to 2 inches of beads. These can be beads that match the beads on the edge of the beadwork, or to introduce new beads. With the beads strung on the thread, move the thread around to determine where to anchor the other end to the middle or other edge of the beadwork. Pass through the bead closest to where you wish to anchor the arch and continue stitching down the row of the beadwork. Add several arches using different types of beads. Stitch back down the side where you just added the arch to begin to build up the arch (**Fig. 2**).

2. Creating a bridge uses the same technique as adding an arch, only you will bring the loose end

Fig. 1

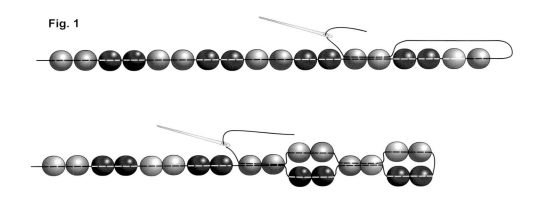

Fig. 2

with the beads over onto the beadwork and anchor the bridge onto the middle portion or other side of the beadwork (**Fig. 3**).

3. Continue stitching back and forth, building up the width of the base beadwork and the arches and bridges until you're satisfied with the appearance. If your lampwork beads are quite large, be sure to add lots of open areas that are captured by arches for balance.

Assembly Instructions

1. Arrange focal beads on design board with largest in center front. On left side, place second large lampwork bead about 2 inches away. Add one smaller lampwork bead about 2 inches away from the second bead. Repeat to arrange right side of necklace. Refer to photo for placement.

2. Thread the needle; double and condition the thread. Add a tension bead to the thread. Start out by adding about 1 inch of each style of the seed beads. If you have a wide variety of sizes, such as 11/0 seed beads and 6/0 beads, plan to stitch the 11/0 beads with double peyote stitch. With this idea, you will want to add the 11/0 seed beads in sets of two beads each.

3. Fill the thread with enough seed beads to create the length of your necklace plus about 1/2 inch of beads. Thread this length through the lampwork beads that are on the beading design board.

4. Begin to stitch the row using double peyote stitch, matching the beads as closely as possible. Stitch back and forth on this row, creating stitched beadwork that looks like small patches of beads joined together end to end. Don't worry about the different bead sizes, it'll all work out.

5. When you reach the lampwork beads, stitch through the seed beads that are going through the holes until they are so full of thread you can't needle through them anymore.

6. After the fourth row, begin to blend the beads into the adjoining patches and add bead arches.

7. When you reach one end of the beadwork, add three seed beads, stitch through one loop on one side of the clasp, add three more seed beads, and stitch back into the beadwork. As the beadwork gets wider as you work, attach the beadwork to the other rings. Repeat to attach the other side of the clasp at the other end.

Fig. 3

Breezy Aqua Basket

Designed by Mary Ayres

Bead stringing and simple wirework unite to embellish this versatile wire basket. This project calls out for your own personal touch of beaded color!

Color Palette

For other cool, refreshing tones, choose your favorite shades of bright blue, light green, or citrine.

Tip

Put a dab of fabric adhesive on the threads that are wrapped around the basket loops to keep them securely in place.

Dimensions
Approximately 10 inches square

Materials
- Wire basket of your choice
- 1 package of ¼ inch glass bugle beads—
  silver-lined turquoise
- 1 package mixed beads—teal
- 1 package mother-of-pearl
  nugget beads
- 1 package brown-lip nugget shells
- 1 package cowrie shell beads
- 32 eye pins, 1¼ inches long—silver
- 12 eye pins, 2 inches long—silver
- 12 jump rings, 7 mm—silver
- Permanent fabric adhesive

Additional Supplies
Basic beading supplies

For product information, see page 124.

Fig. 1

Instructions
1. Thread a beading needle with 36 inches of Silamide and knot it around a corner metal loop on the basket.

2. String enough turquoise bugles to reach the next loop on the basket. Wrap thread through basket loop, and then pass back through the loop twice to secure it. Continue stringing bugles on the basket in the same manner until the strand of beads goes all the way around the basket. If you run out of thread, attach a new piece with a surgeon's knot (see Technique Guide, page 114) and continue. Knot thread ends together at beginning and ending. To hide thread ends, insert needle back through several beads on the string and secure with a knot.

3. Repeat step 2 to make a second strand of beads around the basket, adding several beads to each section so that the strand has a small drape.

4. Repeat step 2 to make a third strand of beads around the basket, adding several more beads to each section so that the strand has a larger drape. Put a dab of fabric adhesive on the threads that are wrapped around the basket loops.

5. Open a jump ring (see Technique Guide, page 114) and slide on a cowrie shell and an eye pin. Close jump ring. Place assorted teal, nugget, and shell beads in a pleasing pattern on a 2-inch-long eye pin. (Beads should cover approximately 1 to 1¼ inches of the eye pin.) Use chain nose pliers to bend eye pin approximately ⅜ inch from the top. Insert eye pin through a metal loop on basket and then continue making a loop using the round nose pliers (**Fig. 1**).

6. Repeat step 5, attaching eye pins through all the loops, except the corners. *Note*: I wanted my beads to hang symmetrically, so I used the same bead assembly for the center droplets, and then changed the bead assembly for the droplets on both sides of the center.

7. Place assorted small teal beads on 1¼-inch-long eye pins. Bend eye pins approximately ⅜ inch from the top using chain nose pliers. Place eye pin over a lower edge on the basket, and then continue making a loop using the round nose pliers. Position beaded eye pins in each lower section on the basket.

Tools:
Chain nose pliers

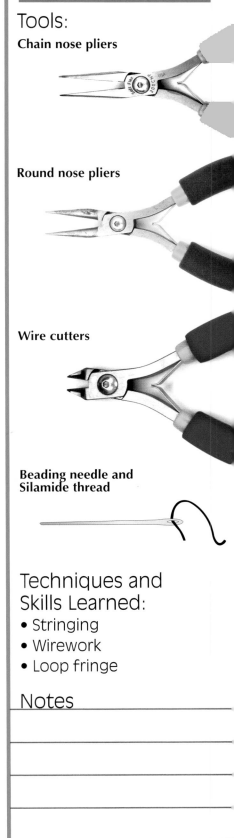

Round nose pliers

Wire cutters

Beading needle and Silamide thread

Techniques and Skills Learned:
- Stringing
- Wirework
- Loop fringe

Notes

Jewelry

Spring Green Dichroic Sparkle Set

Designed by Paula Radke
for Paula Radke Dichroic Beads

Basic stringing and complementary design concepts will allow you to create this sweet, spring-colored necklace, while a couple of wire wrapped loops are all that you'll need to make the matching earrings.

Color Palette
Experiment with beads in ruby, amber, teal, blue, and lavender.

Dimensions
18 inches long

Materials
- 2 rhomboid dichroic beads—apple green over black
- 2 twist dichroic beads—apple green over black
- 3 round dichroic beads, 12mm—apple green core
- 1 round dichroic bead, 12mm—apple green over black
- 18 to 20 inches of 19-strand beading wire
- 64 Chinese fire-polished AB crystals, 6mm—spring green
- 56 Bali spacer beads—silver (optional: Chinese pewter reproductions)
- Toggle clasp—silver
- 2 head pins with ball ends, 2 inches long—silver
- 2 ear wires—silver
- 2 crimp tubes—silver

Additional Supplies
Basic beading supplies, bead design board

For product information, see page 124.

Instructions
Necklace
1. String a crimp tube and half the toggle clasp onto one end of the wire. Pass back through the crimp tube and crimp the tube to secure.

2. Referring to the photo, alternately string 6mm crystals and silver spacer beads until you have strung 25 crystals.

3. On the bead board, arrange the dichroic beads in a pleasing order. String the first dichroic bead, one crystal, one spacer, and one crystal. Repeat this combination six more times.

4. String on the remaining 25 crystals, adding a spacer between each.

5. Finish off with the crimp tube and the other half of the toggle clasp as in step 1.

Earrings
1. Slide a 6mm crystal, a 12mm apple green core dichroic bead, and another 6mm crystal onto each head pin.

2. Make a wrapped or plain loop at the top of each bead group (see Technique Guide, page 114). Attach each beaded head pin to an ear wire.

Tools:
Chain nose pliers

Crimping pliers

Round nose pliers

Wire cutters

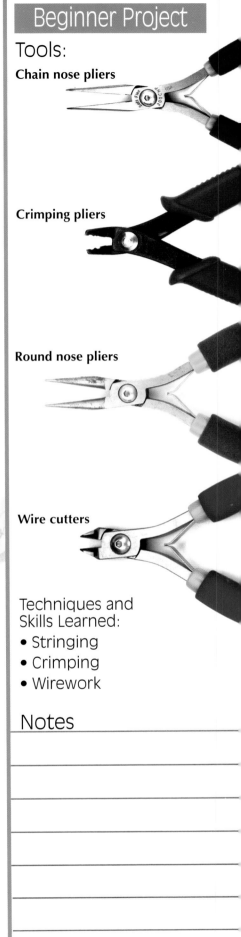

Techniques and Skills Learned:
- Stringing
- Crimping
- Wirework

Notes

Savannah Flower Brooch

Designed by Cynthy Anderson

Bead embroidery at its best! Create an heirloom-quality brooch using a needle and thread, delicate ribbon, lace appliqué, crystals, and seed beads.

Tools:

Size 9 or 10 beading needle and Silamide beading thread

Sewing needle and heavy cotton thread

Beading scissors

Techniques and Skills Learned:
- Stringing
- Bead embroidery:
  Backstitch
  Bead stacks
  Fringing
- Ribbon embroidery:
  Running stitch
  Backstitch

Notes

Tips
- If you find your yo-yo is not as fully beaded as you would like, go back to spaced areas and add as much as desired.
- You may want to experiment with different size beads or add small crystals to your beading and couching techniques.
- Add pressed and vintage beads for a more dimensional and tactile work.

Dimensions
Approximately 6½ x 5 inches

Materials
- 5½-inch-square piece of velvet for pin back
- 4-inch x 12-inch piece of velvet for yo-yos
- Hand-dyed lace appliqué
- 18-inch piece of 1-inch-wide silk ribbon—green
- 1 tube size 11/0 seed beads—ruby silver-lined
- 1 tube size 11/0 seed beads—mauve
- 1 tube size 11/0 seed beads—orange
- 1 tube small bugle beads—orange
- 7 bicones—iridescent mauve
- 5 cathedral-cut beads—green
- 10 teardrop beads—mauve
- 1 pin back

Additional Supplies
Basic beading supplies, fiberfill, pencil, 2½-inch canning jar lid, straight pins, tracing paper

For product information, see page 124.

Instructions

1. Trace the yo-yo pattern onto tracing paper, and cut out and pin to the velvet piece. Cut out the yo-yo shape from velvet.

2. Using the heavy cotton thread and sewing needle, sew a running stitch around the edge of the yo-yo, pull to slightly gather, stuff with fiberfill, and then pull gathers to close. Backstitch to secure.

3. Make a total of three velvet yo-yos.

4. *General yo-yo beading.* Bead the yo-yo using the bead and embroidery backstitching technique (see Technique Guide, page 114). With knotted thread, come through the bottom of yo-yo to the top. Pick up three beads, backstitch into fabric of yo-yo, and come in the back of the second bead. Pass back through second and third bead, needle in front of bead, and pick up three more beads. Repeat around the yo-yo.

Yo-yo #1

1. Bring needle up through base of the yo-yo and stitch ruby seed beads with backstitch as described earlier, working from the center area down to the bottom of the yo-yo (**Fig. 1**). Come back up next to the starting point and repeat across entire outer area of yo-yo. Leave a small round space on the top of the yo-yo unbeaded.

2. To add small beaded loops to the yo-yo center top, bring needle up through center, pick up five ruby seeds, and bring needle back down next to where the thread is coming out. Go back through to bottom of yo-yo and repeat until center is full and you are satisfied with it.

Yo-yo #2

1. Using mauve seeds, refer to photo and backstitch across center of yo-yo in a curved motion for six rows (**Fig. 2**).

2. On unbeaded sides, add bead loops. Pick up five mauve seeds, and pass back through the yo-yo next to the thread on top of yo-yo to bottom of yo-yo.

Yo-yo #3

1. Using orange bugle beads, backstitch horizontally around outer edge of yo-yo, leaving top center open (**Fig. 3**). Secure threads as you go.

2. To add bead stacks in center of yo-yo, pass through a small bugle, add one orange seed, and pass back through the bugle. Bring thread down through fabric at base of bugle and repeat to fill circle.

Brooch back

1. Place the canning lid in the center of the 5½-inch-square piece of velvet, and mark off ½-inch seam allowance around the lid edge.

2. Using knotted thread and the sewing needle, sew a running stitch following the ½-inch seam allowance.

3. Place the lid in the center, pull to gather the velvet, and sew gathered fabric together. The silk ribbon flowers will be attached on this side.

4. Pin lace appliqué approximately ½ inch off the edge on the gathered lid side; sew to secure.

5. Sew pin back to back of velvet lid.

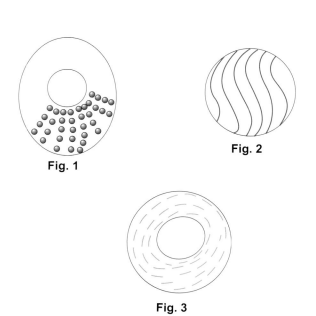

Fig. 1

Fig. 2

Fig. 3

Fig. 4

Fig. 5   Fig. 6

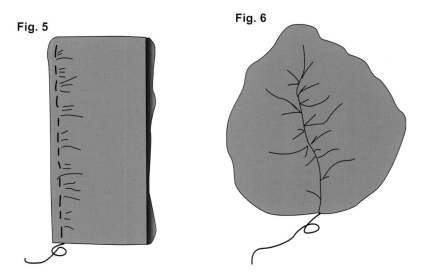

Making large leaves

1. Cut three 6-inch lengths of green ribbon. Fold each 6-inch length in half to make a 3-inch x 1-inch doubled piece.

2. Start a running stitch at the fold of the ribbon, making sure you are stitching both edges along the 3-inch side (**Fig. 4**).

3. Pull the running stitch to gather when you reach the end of the ribbon. Backstitch to secure (**Fig. 5**).

4. Open leaf and finger press so it stays open (**Fig. 6**).

5. Repeat steps 2 through 4 to finish two more leaves.

Assembling the brooch

1. Sew leaves to brooch back, keeping leaf points placed outward (refer to photo for placement).

2. Secure all three beaded yo-yos to the velvet with sewing thread. Refer to photo for placement.

Fringe

1. To make the side fringe, knot the end of 24 inches of beading thread and come up through back to front of the lace appliqué, referring to photo for location. Secure with a knot.

2. Pick up two mauve seeds, a bicone, a mauve seed, a teardrop, a mauve seed, a cathedral-cut bead, a mauve seed, a teardrop, a mauve seed, a bicone, and three mauve seeds. Pass through the lace appliqué and do several backstitches to secure.

3. Weave needle to other side of lace appliqué and repeat step 2.

4. To make the center drop fringe, string two mauve seeds, a bicone, a mauve seed, a teardrop, a mauve seed, a cathedral-cut bead, a mauve seed, a teardrop, and a mauve seed. Skip the last seed, pass back through all the beads, and secure to lace.

5. Make two more center drop fringes in the same manner, one on each side of the fringe created in step 4.

A little more ribbon and some amazing bead stacks and this brooch says Luxurious!

Clever Conversations!
Cell Phone Cases

Designed by Lisa Swenson Ruble

Instead of embellishing your *cell phone* with crystals, use bead embroidery to decorate a case or two to carry it.

Tips

• If the phone case you purchase is different from these, use that fabric pattern as inspiration for your beading.

• Don't bead the back or the strap of the case, since these areas will experience the most wear and put stress on the beads and thread.

• It isn't necessary to pass all the way through the fabric each time. As long as the needle passes through enough fabric to hold the thread, you're set.

• For more information on couching, see the Technique Guide on page 114.

Dot Crazy Case Materials

• Soft cell phone case—white with green/blue dots
• 1 strand fire-polished crystals—lime green/blue
• 1 strand large faceted beads—turquoise
• 1 strand donut beads—light turquoise
• 1 strand round beads—light green
• 1 tube size 11/0 seed beads—aqua satin
• 1 tube size 11/0 seed beads—dark aqua silver-lined
• 1 tube size 11/0 seed beads—green light matte AB

Tropical Floral Case Materials

• Soft cell phone case—brown with pink flowers
• 1 strand flower beads—light pink
• 1 tube size 8/0 seed beads—amber/brown lined

Additional Supplies

Basic beading supplies

For product information, see page 124.

Dot Crazy Case Instructions

1. *Bead stacks.* Use a variety of beads—seeds, donuts, fire-polished crystals, faceted, and round beads—to make bead stacks on selected dots on the case: thread a needle with about 2 feet of thread and knot the end. Bring the needle up through one of the top dots, string a few beads, skip the top bead, and pass back through the remaining beads into the fabric. Knot the thread to secure the stack and pass needle through the fabric to reach the next dot. *Note:* It's easiest to start with a dot near the top and work down the case rather than sticking your fingers in the case. Referring to the photo, make a variety of bead stacks, including multiple fringes in one dot.

2. *Beaded circles.* Couch a row of seed beads around the outside edge of some of the dots.

3. *First row of fringe.* Bring a threaded needle out at the seam where the case begins to round at the bottom. String three dark aqua seeds, one light green round bead, and three dark aqua seeds. Pass through the fabric, knot to secure, and bring needle out next to the first fringe. Repeat across the bottom edge of the case.

4. *Second row of fringe.* Position needle behind the first row of the fringe. String five aqua satin seeds, one lime green/blue fire-polished crystal, and five more aqua satin seeds. Pass through the fabric, knot to secure, and bring needle out next to the first fringe. Repeat across the bottom edge of the case.

Tropical Floral Case Instructions

1. Thread needle with 2 feet of beading thread and knot the end. Bring thread up from the inside of the case, near the top. String five to six amber seeds, pass back through the fabric, and couch the beads in place (see Technique Guide, page 114). Use amber seeds and a couching technique to fill in the center of the flower pattern, covering all brown space.

2. Bring the needle up through the flower center and string a light pink flower bead above the seed bead base. Add three to five amber seeds, skip the last seed, and pass back through all beads back into fabric. Repeat two more times to create a dimensional flower center. Secure thread and trim end.

3. Start another thread and bring out at seam on the lower right corner of the case. Create a piece of fringe by stringing a combination of six to 10 amber seeds and a pink flower bead. Skip the last bead and pass through all beads back into the fabric. Knot to secure and begin another piece of fringe. Make about ten pieces of fringe of varying lengths and bead combinations.

Beginner Project

Tools:

Beading needle and nylon beading thread

Beading scissors

Techniques and Skills Learned:
- Bead embroidery:
    Stacks
    Couching
    Fringe

Notes

Jewelry

Grapetini Necklace
& Earrings

Designed by Kelly Wilson

Basic crochet stitches create the foundation for
this set, while seed bead embellishment evokes thoughts
of sugar-encrusted martini glasses
and long conversations with good friends.

Tips

• A skein of yarn is approximately 250 yards.
• Gauge: from crocheted pearl to next crocheted pearl =
3 inches (crocheted only, no beads added).
• This necklace can be made in many lengths. Lengthen the necklace by repeating
steps 2 and 3 more than 10 times until desired length is reached. Likewise, shorten
the necklace by repeating steps 2 and 3 fewer than 10 times.
• Make many lengths in delicious colors. Like Grapetinis, you can't have just one!

Materials

• 12 yards of Bamboo yarn—plum
• 2 packages each of size 11/0 seed beads—cranberry gold luster, deep magenta
lined AB, and raspberry luster
• 2 earring wires—gold

Additional Supplies

Basic beading supplies, teaspoon

For product information, see page 124.

Dimensions

Necklace: 30 inches
Earrings: 1½ inches

Necklace Instructions

Crochet

   Note: These instructions assume basic crocheting knowledge. See the
Technique Guide on p. 114 for a glossary of crochet stitches.
   1. Make slip knot and ch 10, sl st into first ch to create loop for closure (**Fig. 1**).
   2. Ch 10, add 1 dc into third ch from hook (**Fig. 2**).
   3. Ch 10, add 5 dc into third ch from hook (**Fig. 3**), carefully remove hook from
last loop, insert hook into first dc (**Fig. 4**), and pull last loop through to create a
pearl (**Fig. 5**).
   4. Repeat steps 2 and 3 to desired length.
   5. Fasten off. Using a needle with a large hole, weave in ends. *Note:* The two
ends will be attached together later.

Beading

   1. Mix a teaspoon of each color of the Seed Beads in the bead dish.
   2. Thread beading needle with 18 inches of thread and anchor approximately ⅛
inch from one end of a crocheted pearl, add five beads from the mix, and push
needle into edge of pearl (**Fig. 6**). Come up through pearl and pass through last
three placed beads to couch into place (see Technique Guide, page 114). Continue
in this manner around crocheted pearl.

Tools:

Size B/1 (2.5mm) crochet hook

Needle with large eye

**Size 10 beading needle and
size B nylon beading thread**

Techniques and Skills Learned:

• Crochet stitches:
   Chain stitch
   Double crochet stitch
• Stringing
• Bead embellishment

Notes

3. Create a second ring of beads, in the same manner as in step 2, at outer edge of previous ring of beads.

4. Create a third ring of beads around outermost edge of crocheted pearl, adding three beads at a time. Couch by coming up through last two beads placed. Keeping the chained length in the center of this last ring, insert beading needle through crocheted pearl to its opposite end (**Fig. 7**).

5. Bead the opposite end of crocheted pearl as explained in steps 2 to 4.

6. Repeat steps 2 to 5 for each crocheted pearl (**Fig. 8**).

7. Thread beading needle with 10 inches of thread, and anchor it to 1 dc in ch. Add five beads from the mix, and push needle back through opposite end of dc to make the center line of beads (**Fig. 9**).

8. Bring up needle next to center line of beads. Add three beads, and push needle back through opposite end of dc.

9. Repeat step 8 on opposite side of center line of beads.

10. Repeat steps 7 to 9 for other side of 1 dc section to cover front and back with beads (**Fig. 10**).

11. Cut a 35-inch length of thread. Secure it to sl st at loop for necklace closure. Add 17 beads from mix. Insert beading needle into closest end of first ball, through its center, and out the other end of ball.

12. Add 17 beads. Insert beading needle into next ball and through its center, exiting at the opposite end.

13. Repeat step 12 along the length of necklace.

14. Cut two more 35-inch lengths of thread. Secure each one to sl st at loop for necklace closure slightly to one side of the original length in step 11. Place beads along length of necklace as explained in steps 11 to 13 (**Fig. 11**).

Earring Instructions

Crochet

1. Make slip knot and ch 5, dc in third ch from hook.

2. Ch 6, 5 dc in third ch from hook, carefully remove hook from last loop, insert hook into first dc, and pull last loop through to create pearl.

3. Fasten off. Using needle with large hole, weave in ends.

4. Repeat steps 1 to 3 for second earring.

Beading

1. Bead earring piece in the same way done for the necklace.

2. Attach beginning ch to wire loop of earring wire.

3. Repeat steps 1 and 2 for second earring.

Fig. 1

Fig. 2

Fig. 3

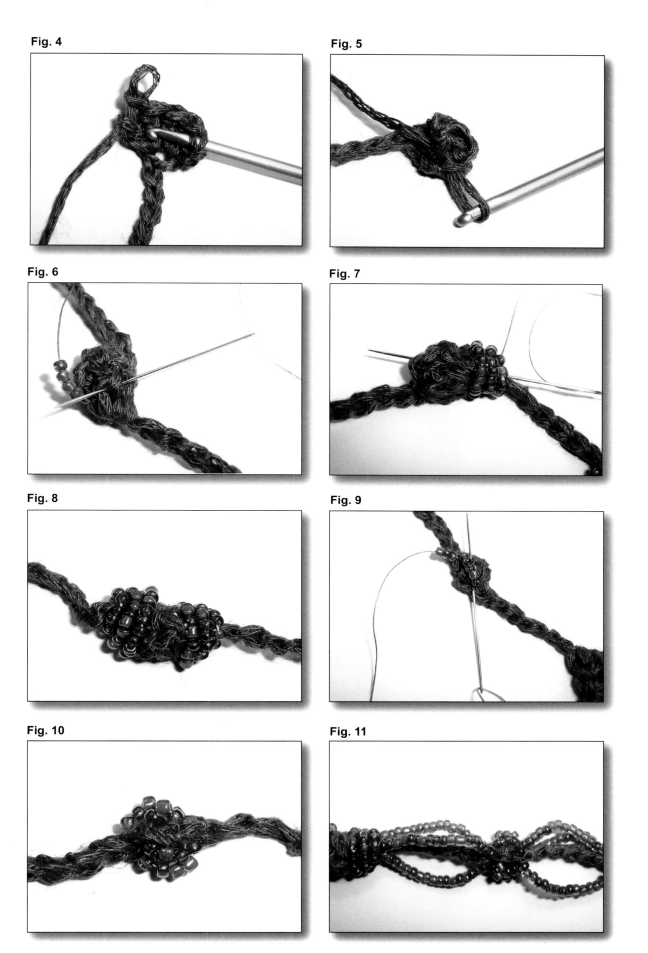

Fig. 4

Fig. 5

Fig. 6

Fig. 7

Fig. 8

Fig. 9

Fig. 10

Fig. 11

Rockin' Jewelry

Designed by
Barbara Matthiessen

Exercise your wire working skills by encasing collected river or beach stones from a special trip in silver wire—you'll want to showcase every found object you can!

Inspiration

Gaze into a stream bottom or look at beach stones lapped by the water and you will see glorious colors and patterns. I remember lifting stones out of the water, sticking them in my pocket, and carrying them home only to be disappointed by their lackluster appearance once dry. Later, I learned people used tumblers and grits and polishes to maintain that "in the water" look.

I was determined to find a way to get the same results in less time. After experimenting, I came up with the a method to get the same shiny effect—acrylic glaze to the rescue! Coat each stone with acrylic glaze, let dry, and you are done in an afternoon.

Tips

• The shinier the varnish, the harder protective finish it leaves.
• To make necklaces or bracelets, choose a variety of colored stones that are smooth and have a flat back. Use bicone-shaped or triangular stones for earrings, pendants, and brooches.
• Choose stones no larger than 3⁄4 inch for necklaces and bracelets and 1⁄2 inch for earrings to minimize the weight.
• Collect stones from a special trip or occasion to make an especially meaningful piece.
• Coat more stones than you need, so you can pick and choose as you construct the jewelry.
• Allow each side coated with the high-gloss acrylic glaze to dry completely before coating second side or starting to wire wrap.
• Whenever possible, work wire off the spool to give leverage for making wraps and to save wire.
• Use side-cutters to trim wires closely, sand rough ends, and then press wires down to prevent snags.
• Try using different colors of wire to wrap or string your stones and beads.

Tools:

Chain nose pliers

Round nose pliers

Flush cutters

Wire file

Techniques and Skills Learned:
• Wirework:
   Wire wrapping
   Wire shaping

Notes

Dimensions
Vary based on size and quantity of stones

Materials
For All Projects
- High-gloss thick acrylic glaze (brush-on or aerosol spray)—clear
- 6 yards of 22-gauge non-tarnish silver wire
- 5-inch square piece of screening or other non-stick surface

For Necklace
- 14 stones of choice
- 26 barrel beads, 8mm x 6mm—silver
- 12 spacer beads, 7mm x 6mm—silver
- Toggle closure—silver

For Earrings
- 2 stones of choice
- 4 barrel beads, 8mm x 6mm—silver
- 2 earring findings—silver

For Key Ring Dangle
- Medium stone of choice
- Medium size lanyard hook—silver

Additional Supplies
Basic beading supplies, bead design board, paper towel, ruler, small disposable paintbrush (if using brush-on acrylic glaze), soap and water to clean rocks

For product information, see page 124.

Necklace Instructions

1. Collect and clean stones to remove any surface dirt. Place clean and dry stones on screening. Use paintbrush to coat top side of each stone with high-gloss acrylic glaze or spray on a coat following manufacturer's instructions. Allow this side to dry completely. Turn stones over and coat reverse side with high-gloss acrylic glaze.

2. Start wire wrapping stones by forming a loop with round nose pliers. *Note:* When making loops for this project, wrap wire around the halfway point on the round nose pliers. Twist wire once around base of loop then trim tail to ¼ inch (**Fig. 1**). Hold against backside of stone, allowing the loop to extend past stone edge (**Fig. 2**). Bend wire to opposite end of stone.

Fig. 1   **Fig. 2**

3. Hold wire onto stone while creating a loop at the opposite end of the stone. Wrap wire once around the base of the loop (**Fig. 3**).

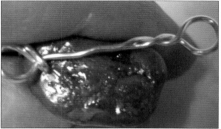

Fig. 3

4. Position wire diagonally and tightly across top of stone and wrap around original loop. Repeat the diagonal wrap, working in the opposite direction to form an "X" across the top of the stone (**Fig. 4**).

Fig. 4

5. Trim and file wire end, and use flat nose pliers to squeeze and harden the wraps. Tuck in wire tail on backside. Repeat steps 2 through 5 to create 10 more wrapped stones for the necklace.

6. Lay stones out on bead design board and plan the necklace arrangement, placing the largest stone in the center surrounded by five stones on each side.

7. To make wire-and-silver-beaded link, form a loop in wire, slide through loop on the wrapped stone, and then wrap wire around first loop base (**Fig. 5**). Add a barrel, spacer, and barrel bead combination to the wire (**Fig. 6**). Cut wire 2 inches from the last barrel bead. Form a loop with the short wire end and slide it through another wrapped stone loop to join. Wrap wire two or three times around loop base. Trim, file, and tuck wire end in.

Fig. 5

Fig. 6

10. Wrap two stones with single loops to attach to sides of center stone. Form a loop and slide one stone onto each loop of the center stone. Wrap wire once around base of loop. Crisscross-wrap wire around stone, bringing wire back to loop and wrapping wire around loop base. Repeat step for second stone.

11. To make the bead/stone drop, form a wire loop and slide around center back wrap on center stone. Wrap short wire end around loop base. Add barrel bead. Hold a stone next to base of barrel bead, and then tightly crisscross-wrap stone with wire. Bring wire to bottom of stone and add a barrel bead. Snug last bead up to base of stone, and form wire loop. Wrap stone and then tuck wire end down into bead.

Earring Instructions

Make two bead/stone drops following instructions in step 7 for the necklace. Attach the loop at one end to earring finding. Repeat for second earring.

8. Connect five wrapped stones to each side of center stone using the beaded-link technique described in step 7.

9. Attach toggle closure to necklace by making a wire link. Form a loop and slide it through the end loop on the last bead link. Wrap wire around base of loop. Cut wire 2 inches from last wire wrap. Form loop and slide on closure piece. Wrap wire around base of loop (**Fig. 7**). Repeat on opposite side to complete closure. Trim and file all wire ends.

Fig. 7

Key Ring Dangle Instructions

1. Choose a single medium stone and make a bead/stone drop following step 7 of the necklace instructions. If desired, use several stones.

2. Attach a lanyard hook or giant jump ring at the top of the dangle.

Key Ring Dangle

Build a Bead Button

Designed by Kim Ballor

Using a simple wire wrapped loop, turn disk-style beads into unique buttons to jazz up any outfit in a hurry. Layer the beads until you achieve the look you like. It's fun and simple!

Tips

• If the button has to be functional, make sure the beads you use can go through the buttonhole.

• If your bead is not perfectly flat, add a flat disc bead to the back of the button. The disc bead should have a small hole. This will stabilize the button, holding all the layers tightly in place.

• To wear the buttons, attach with a button safety pin, available at any fabric store.

• Take the buttons off for washing the garment or for trying out different looks.

Dyed Bone Disc Buttons
Materials for one button

- Green-dyed bone disc bead, 25mm
- Bali spacer bead, 15mm—silver
- Crystal bicone bead, 6mm—green
- Flat disc bead with small hole—any size, any material
- Head pin with flower head—silver
- Button safety pin

Additional Supplies

Basic beading supplies

For product information, see page 124.

Instructions

1. Place beads on head pin as follows: crystal bicone, Bali spacer, dyed bone disc, flat disc. *Note:* The flat disc will stabilize the button by providing a flat bottom and holding all layers together.

2. Tightly wrap a loop on the back of the flat disc using the round nose pliers (see Technique Guide, page 114). Wrap tightly so the beads do not slide on the head pin. Trim excess end of head pin with flush cutters and press flat against wire wrap with chain nose pliers so the cut end will not catch on the garment.

3. Attach to your jacket, shirt, or garment of choice with a button safety pin.

Color Palette

Ready to get wild and crazy with beaded buttons? Use the following suggested material lists for a little variety.

Make each button using the instructions listed above for the Dyed Bone Disc Buttons.

Leaf Buttons
Materials for one button

- Round lampwork disc bead, 17mm—blue
- Glass leaf bead—green
- Head pin with leaf head—silver
- Disc bead with small hole—any size
- Button safety pin

Cube Buttons
Materials for one button

- Lampwork cube bead, 12mm—blue with green dots
- Round Bali spacer bead, 11mm—silver
- Crystal bicone bead, 6mm—blue
- Head pin with ball head—silver
- Button safety pin

Round Buttons
Materials for one button

- Round lampwork bead, 14mm—solid color
- Open half of fancy square toggle—silver
  (clip the loop off with flush cutters)
- Bali spacer bead, 15mm—silver
- Plain bead cap, 4mm—silver
- Flat disc bead with small hole—any size
- Head pin with tiny dangles for head—silver
- Button safety pin

Tools:

Chain nose pliers

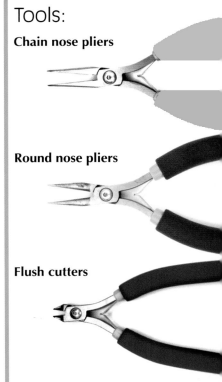

Round nose pliers

Flush cutters

Techniques and Skills Learned:

- Wirework:
  Wire wrapping

Notes

Best Friend's Bracelet

Designed by Eleanore Macnish

Combine **simple stringing** and a little **imagination** to create an **eye-catching bracelet** with cut-glass charms and lampwork glass beads — a **perfect gift for your best friend.**

Tip

This bracelet will work with any kind of lampwork bead; however, to get vibrant colors and clarity, be sure to select top-quality beads.

Dimensions

7 inches long

Materials

• 2 pieces, each 11 inches long, of .024 beading wire
• 4 crimp beads, 2mm—sterling silver
• 140 size 6/0 seed beads—assorted colors
• 5 lampwork or accent beads, 6mm to 10mm
• 2 large endcaps (large enough to hide two crimp beads on each end)
• 2 head pins—silver
• 4 jump rings, 5mm—sterling silver

• 2 jump rings, 8mm—sterling silver
• Toggle clasp—sterling silver
• Various charms, stones, silver spacer beads, and a vintage clip-on rhinestone earring

Additional Supplies

Basic beading supplies

For product information, see page 124.

Instructions

1. Using wire cutters, cut one 11-inch piece of wire. Thread one end through a crimp bead, an end cap, the toggle clasp loop, and back through the end cap and crimp bead. Snug all components together. Crimp the bead with chain nose pliers. (I prefer chain nose pliers to crimping pliers because I always have the feeling that the crimping pliers

leave a crease in the metal and weaken it by doing so.) Make sure the crimp bead is hidden by the end caps.

2. Repeat these steps to attach the second strand of wire (**Fig. 1**).

3. Thread the seed beads and lampwork beads onto the wire until you have about 6¼ inches of beaded wire. Thread the end through a crimp bead and repeat step 1.

4. To create the second strand, string seed beads to make a beaded wire measuring 6¾ inches to 7 inches long. Thread the end through a crimp bead. *Note:* The second beaded strand should be ½ inch to ¾ inch longer than the first. This will create a drape effect.

5. Attaching the charms, stones, and earring is the easy part! To attach the earring to the longest beaded strand, start by removing the long clip arm from the back of the earring. To do this, just splay out the sides of the part holding the clip and slip it out of the holes that hold it in place (**Fig. 2**). Bend the sides back into their original position and place your pliers lengthwise on the metal tab on the back of the earring (**Fig. 3**). Apply even pressure and slowly bend the tab down until the sides touch the back of the earring. *You only have one chance to do this, so be careful.* The metal on vintage earrings will not stand up to being bent more than once. Connect the two 8mm jump rings and slip one of them through the top of the loop you have just created by bending the tab (**Fig. 4**). Close the jump ring. This new earring "charm" can now be attached to the long strand of your bracelet—the jump ring will allow it to slide over the beads.

6. Attach your other charms to the shorter strand. Stack your stones and silver spacer beads of choice on the head pin as desired. Use the round nose pliers to make a wrapped loop above the top stone or bead (see Technique Guide, page 114). Repeat to make a second head pin bauble and attach both to one 5mm jump ring. Use chain nose pliers to connect the bauble to the bracelet. Attach remaining charms to 5mm jump rings and use chain nose pliers to connect them to the bracelet (**Fig. 5**). You're done!! Enjoy your bracelet and your best friend's delight when she receives your gift!

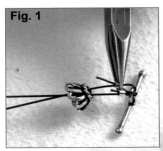

Fig. 1

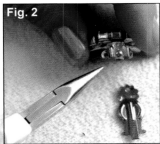

Fig. 2

Fig. 3

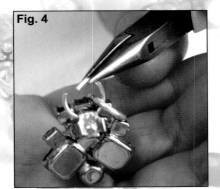

Fig. 4

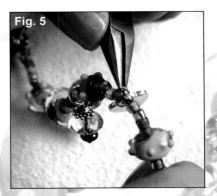

Fig. 5

Bead My Jeans!

A great way to give a pair of jeans pizzazz is to embellish them with beads.
Simple stitches, couching, and some loop fringe make a dramatic difference.

Ladders and Scallops Jeans

Designed by Dorothy Egan

Inspiration

I wanted to dress up my jeans with some fun beaded embroidery. Black and iridescent beads go with almost anything, and I love the look!

Tips

• Couching is an easy and secure way to attach a string of beads onto fabric. This technique allows you to turn and swirl beads in different directions with ease.

• Create a designer look for just pennies—use jeans and beads you already have!

Materials

- Pair of blue jeans
- 610 seed beads—black opal
- 850 bugle beads—black iris
- 40 star and face beads—dark blue iridescent

Additional Supplies

Basic beading supplies

For product information, see page 124.

Instructions

Beading the leg of jeans

1. Using knotted double thread and beading needle, stitch through jeans at side seam 5 inches from bottom cuff to secure. String 28 alternating seed beads and bugle beads onto thread. Place beaded thread across front of jean leg diagonally to hem in desired position (see photo for reference). Keeping thread snug, pass needle through jeans to back. Knot thread.

2. Referring to the Technique Guide on page 114, reverse stitch and couch thread between every one or two beads along your bead row. Knot thread on backside to secure.

3. See **Fig. 1** for a placement diagram for the following steps. Make a second row above the first, using 30 each of seed and bugle beads. Tack in place using the couching technique. Sew bugle beads between the two rows at each seed bead. *Note:* Bugle beads can be sharp at the ends, so place a seed bead at each end of the bugle bead to protect the thread.

4. Use the beading needle and knotted double thread to make the bead scallops. Stitch through jeans below the first seed bead in the bottom row. Beginning with a seed bead, string alternating seed beads and bugle beads onto thread, using four seed beads and three bugle beads. Add a star or face bead, string on another alternating four seed beads and three bugle beads, and sew back through jeans after the ninth bead in bottom row. This forms the loop. Pull thread back through jeans and repeat to make seven loops. Knot thread.

5. Repeat on backside of jean leg and then on the second jean leg.

Beading the pocket

1. Using knotted double thread and the beading needle, stitch through jeans at side seam between the two rows of stitching at the top of the pocket. String alternating seed beads and bugle beads onto thread to span the pocket. Sew through jeans and knot thread.

2. Using a knotted single thread, sew back and forth (couching) across beaded strand at each seed bead to tack strand in place. Make loops hanging below the bead strand as described in step 4 above.

Washing instructions: Due to the delicate nature of beaded embroidery, hand wash these jeans and hang to dry.

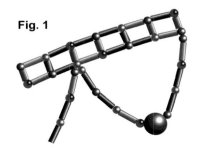

Fig. 1

Fall Flower Jeans

Designed by Lisa Swenson Ruble

Inspiration

The fibers I chose for this project suggest fall foliage to me. What better way to hold onto summer a little longer than to create beautiful summer flowers in harvest colors? The flowers and foliage together create a fresh look to keep those chilly fall days at bay.

Tips

• Only trace one design element at a time because the ink can disappear faster than you can stitch!
• Couch beads as often as necessary to retain design shape and secure beads.
• For more information on couching, see the Technique Guide on p. 114.
• When a thread runs out, knot the end securely and begin a new thread.

Materials

- Pair of bootleg jeans
- Fibers—vegetation green
- 1 tube of size 11/0 seed beads—ruby
- 1 tube of bugle beads—ruby
- 40 size 12/0 seed beads—turquoise
- 1 package of faceted beads—multicolor

Additional Supplies

Basic beading supplies, fine point disappearing ink marker pen

Instructions

1. Trace the starburst flower pattern onto a piece of tracing paper with a pencil. Using scissors, cut around the pattern, leaving about ¼ inch above the tip of each starburst line. Referring to the photo for placement, pin the flower pattern to one jean leg or sketch the pattern freehand onto the jean leg using the disappearing ink marking pen.

2. Thread the beading needle with 36 inches of nylon beading thread, double it, and knot the end. Bring the thread up from inside the jeans along the outline of the flower's center. String on four to six ruby seed beads or bugles, lay beads along the nearest starburst outline, and go back through jeans after the last bead. Bring the needle up again on the outline near the middle of the string of beads, loop over the thread between the beads, and pass back into the jeans, pulling tight. *Note:* Always begin and end the row with a ruby seed bead. Vary the number of seed beads and bugle beads used along each starburst line.

3. Continue this couching process, using the pattern as a guide, until each starburst line is beaded. If the pattern was pinned to the jean leg, carefully remove the tracing paper from the stitches. If the pattern was sketched using the disappearing ink pen, the ink should now be invisible.

4. Create the center by stitching a line of four turquoise faceted beads. Add two lines of turquoise seed beads below the main cluster for pollen.

5. Using the photo as a guide, draw the leaves around the beaded flower with the disappearing ink pen. Cut a length of two green fibers about 5 in. long. Place the fibers together on the leaf outline and whip stitch over them to secure (see Technique Guide, p. 114). *Note:* Make several anchor stitches near the end of the fiber to protect it from fraying. Continue whip stitching along the outline, adjusting

Use similar techniques to further embellish your jeans

the fibers to create the leaf shape. Cut and attach another short piece of fiber to create the vein. Repeat for remaining leaves.

6. Sketch the vine onto the jean leg with the disappearing ink pen, making sure the vine touches each leaf. Choose the thickest fiber to be the vine, and tack it down as in step 5.

7. Add two filler flowers using four faceted beads each—one in purple and one in yellow. Stitch in a center with a bead of choice.

8. Repeat steps 1-7 to bead the second jean leg.

Washing instructions: Because of the delicate nature of the beads, the fiber, and the thread holding it all together, handwash these jeans and let them air dry.

Contrasting Tangents Embellished Neck Ring

Designed by Lynda Musante

Learn unique wire manipulation and create "wire curl" head pins while completing this unusual necklace combining crystal and matte finish lampwork beads.

Inspiration
My challenge was to combine sparkling crystal beads with beautiful matte finish lampwork glass to create a lightweight necklace that shines the focus on the beads.

Tip
Carefully file the wire ends to ensure they are smooth and won't snag clothing or scratch skin.

Dimensions
18 inches embellished

Materials
• 16 lampwork glass beads—complementary in color, size, and shape
• 8 cube crystals—crystal AB
• 8 sequin shaped crystals—crystal AB
• 16 size 11/0 seed beads—colors to complement the lampwork
• 30 inches of 20-gauge wire—silver plated
• 18 inches neck ring with bayonet-style clasp—sterling silver

Additional Supplies
Basic beading supplies

For product information, see on page 124.

Instructions

1. Cut a 6-inch length of wire and file both ends. Make a tiny loop on one end using the tips of the round nose pliers (see Technique Guide, page 114). Rotate the pliers and begin to create a flat spiral. Switch to the chain nose pliers and continue building the spiral for three rotations (**Fig. 1a**).

2. Using the chain nose pliers, make a right angle bend in the wire at the base of the spiral and bend the wire down across the back of the spiral (**Fig. 1b**). Firmly flatten the wire across the back of the spiral. Grip the bent wire and the spiral and bend the wire up at a right angle (**Fig. 1c**).

3. Add a lampwork bead, a seed bead, and a cube bead (bead set 1). Next, add a sequin bead, a seed bead, and a lampwork bead (bead set 2). *Note:* Make sure the lampwork beads differ in color and size for interest. Slide all beads to the spiral end of the wire and repeat step 2 to create and position a spiral on the other end of the wire.

4. Repeat steps 1 through 3 with the remaining beads to create eight bead-and-wire elements, each consisting of a bead set 1 and a bead set 2.

5. Separate the bead sets on a bead-and-wire element so that three beads are positioned up against a spiral at each end. Position the end lampwork bead on the base of the twist-n'-curl tool so the rest of the bead-and-wire element extends down the tool's mandrel (**Fig. 2**). Hold the bead in place with one hand and use your other hand to wrap the wire around the mandrel between the bead sets as shown in **Fig. 4**, making sure the wraps are not too close together. Repeat with all of the wire and bead elements.

6. Place the bead-and-wire element with the largest bead on it against the center front of the neck ring (**Fig. 3**). Starting about ¼ to ½ inch from the bead at one end, wrap the coiled wire around the neck ring, stopping about ¼ to ½ inch before the bead on the other end of the bead-and-wire element. Repeat with the bead-and-wire element that has the second largest lampwork bead (**Fig. 4**). It is okay to overlap wires as you twist.

7. Continue adding bead-and-wire elements, varying the sizes and colors as you go. Bend the wire so the beads are positioned up, down, and facing forward to create dimension.

Intermediate Project

Tools:

Chain nose pliers

Flat metal file

Round nose pliers

Wire cutters

Mini Twist N' Curl Tool

Techniques and Skills Learned:
• Wirework:
Wire shaping
Creating wire spirals

Notes

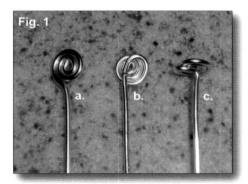

Fig. 1

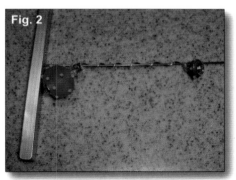

Fig. 2

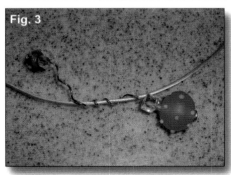

Fig. 3

Fig. 4

Beaded Wine Glasses

**Designed by
Nicole Campanella**

Master peyote stitch while you turn a plain
wine glass into a beaded masterpiece.
Bead entire sets to match your
own china or create gifts
your friends will love!

Inspiration

Fourteen years ago, I was in Oklahoma for the birth of my first grandchild. A young woman commented on a beaded barrette I was wearing, and soon our conversation shifted to creative ideas for beaded tableware. After I returned home, I began beading on wine glass stems, and I have been creating sets for wedding gifts and bridal and specialty shops ever since.

Tips

• Turn short-stemmed glasses upside down to make them easier to bead.
• Before beading, wash the glasses in warm, sudsy water using mild liquid dish soap; dry with a dish towel. After beading, wash again by hand. *Do not wash in dishwasher.*

Materials

• Wine glasses, preferably with a 3-inch or longer stem
• 1 tube each of size 11/0 seed beads—matte lavender iris; blacklined dark green; frosted white
• 1 tube of 3mm glass rounds to match seed beads

Additional Supplies

Basic beading supplies, beeswax

For product information, see page 124.

A word about wine glasses

Although you purchase wine glasses in a set, they may not all be the same size. During the cooling process, glass expands at different rates, even in a mold, cooling at slightly different diameters. Once you start beading, you may find that one stem is actually larger than the other. My remedy for this is to start each glass somewhere in the middle of the stem with the same amount of starting beads. You will be increasing and decreasing up and down the stem anyway, so forget about the bead count.

Another suggestion is either to bead the wine glasses in one color or in designs that move the eye, such as overlapping lines, spirals, a menagerie of flowers, or 3-D boxes. No one will ever know that one glass has more beads than another.

Instructions
Increasing and decreasing

Increasing and decreasing on the stem is a matter of knowing your work. When beads are spaced far apart, it is time to increase by one bead. Don't increase too many times or your beadwork will not fit tightly on the stem. The same goes for decreasing: make the decrease before your work becomes loose on the stem and beads are too close together.

Tools:

Size 12 beading needle and size B nylon beading thread

Beading scissors

Techniques and Skills Learned:

• Bead weaving:
    Peyote stitch
    Netting
    Picot stitch

Notes

There are several approaches to accomplish the increase and decrease steps. Here is how I did them for this project:

1. To increase, string two seed beads instead of one and pass through the next bead (**Fig. 1**). Continue around.

2. When you reach the increase beads, peyote into the first bead as usual. Find a thin bead and peyote in between the two increase beads (**Fig. 2**). Peyote into the next bead on the row and continue around. Peyote the following row as usual.

3. To decrease, peyote until you reach the place to decrease. Pass through two beads instead of one (**Fig. 3**), and continue the row.

4. On the next row when you come to the two beads, peyote over them as if they are one bead (**Fig. 4**). Continue the row.

Starting the glass stem

1. Begin with the traditional peyote start up. String enough seed beads to fit around the middle of the glass stem. You want the two end beads to just touch, but do not overlap.

2. Remove half of the total bead count. If you have an odd number of beads, leave the extra bead strung. String that number of beads in the pattern. For instance, if the bead count is ten, string three lavender, two green, three lavender, and two green (**Fig. 5**).

3. Slide the beads to the tail end of the thread and pass back through all the beads to form a circle. Place the circle of beads onto the glass stem. Pull the thread so beads are snug. Following the thread direction, pass through beads with the tail. Don't worry about evenly spacing the beads; that will happen when you start the next row. Work toward the base of the glass.

4. String one bead and pass through the next bead. (Do not skip any beads on the foundation row.) Following the pattern, repeat around the row, stepping down at the last bead.

5. Continue to peyote, increasing where needed until you reach the very end of the stem. The last row of beads should just be touching the base of the glass.

Bottom base lacing

Row 1. Peyote with white beads.

Row 2. Using a two-bead pick up, peyote with white beads, stepping down and exiting through the first white bead of the first set of two sewn on (**Fig.6**).

Row 3. String three white beads and pass through the first bead of the next set (**Fig. 7**). Repeat around the row, stepping down and exiting through the first two white beads of the first set of three sewn on.

Row 4. String two green beads and pass through the first two white beads of the next set (**Fig. 8**). Continue around the row, stepping down and exiting from the first green bead in the first set of two sewn on.

Row 5. String four green beads and pass through the first bead of the next set of two green beads (**Fig. 9**). Continue around the row, stepping down and exiting from the first two green beads of the first set of four green beads sewn on.

Row 6. String five lavender beads and pass through the first two green beads on the next set of four green beads (**Fig. 10**). Continue around the row, stepping down and exiting from the middle point bead of the first set of lavender sewn on.

Row 7. String seven beads: two lavender, one green, one white, one green, and two lavender (**Fig. 11**). Pass through the next point bead. Continue around the row, stepping down and exiting from the white point bead.

Row 8. Pick up seven beads: two white, three green, and two white (**Fig. 11**). Pass through the next white point bead. Continue around the row, stepping down and exiting from the green point bead.

Row 9. Working off the green point beads, string two green, one lavender, one white, one 3mm lavender, one white, one lavender, and two green beads (**Fig. 11**). Continue around the row. Weave thread into work and trim excess.

Fig. 1

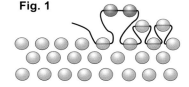

Fig. 2

Fig. 3

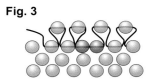

Fig. 4

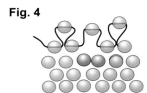

Fig. 5

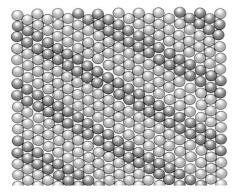

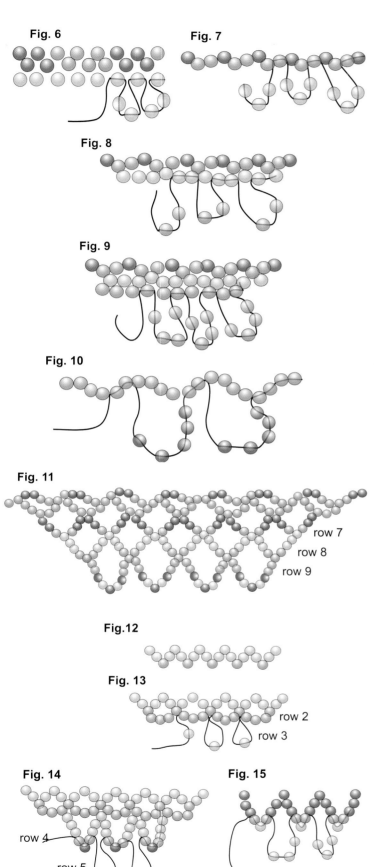

Fig. 6

Fig. 7

Fig. 8

Fig. 9

Fig. 10

Fig. 11

row 7
row 8
row 9

Fig.12

Fig. 13

row 2
row 3

Fig. 14

row 4
row 5

Fig. 15

Beading the stem top

1. With a new thread, weave needle to exit any bead in the stem foundation row.

2. Continue to peyote, following the pattern up the step toward the cup. You may need to decrease and increase as you bead.

3. After reaching the top of the stem, continue to peyote a few more rows. The last row of beads should be spaced as if it needs an increase. This is where the top lacing begins.

Top lacing

Peyote two rows of white beads. The beads should have wide spaces between them.

Row 1. String one white, one green, one white, and peyote into the next bead (**Fig. 12**). Continue this pattern around the row, exiting from the first green point bead.

Row 2. String three green beads and pass through the next green point bead (**Fig. 13**). Continue around the row, exiting from all three green beads first sewn on.

Row 3. String one white bead and pass through all three of the next set of green beads. Do not fit the white bead between the green beads; the white bead sits above the green (**Fig. 13**).

Row 4. Working out of the white beads, pick up two white, one green, one lavender, one green, and two white and pass through the next white bead (**Fig. 14**). Follow this pattern around the row, exiting from the top green, lavender, and green beads.

Row 5. Pick up one 3mm lavender bead and pass through the next set of green, lavender, and green beads (**Fig. 14**). Follow this pattern around the row. *Note:* At this point the lace should lie flat against the cup of the glass. If it doesn't, replace the 3mm bead with a seed bead. This should pull it together.

Row 6. With the needle exiting the 3mm bead, string two lavender, one green, one white, one green, and two lavender. pass through the next 3mm bead (**Fig. 15**). Continue around the row.

Row 7. Connect row 6 by passing through the green, white, and green beads. String three white beads and pass through the next set of green, white, and green beads. Continue around the row.

Depending on the pitch of the glass, you may want to continue the lacing. At some point the beads will not hold up, and the lacing will become heavy and slide down the cup.

Embellishing the stem

1. Starting at the last row of lavender and green seed beads, weave your needle so it exits any of the middle lavender seed beads.

2. String one white, one 3mm lavender, one white bead, and peyote into the next bead.

3. Skip three beads in the lavender spiral and add another grouping of beads. Continue to the bottom of the glass.

4. Weave your thread into your work and trim excess.

Desert Blue Bracelet

Designed by Susan Barnes

Bead stringing and crimping are all that you'll need to put together this bright, Native American-themed bracelet.

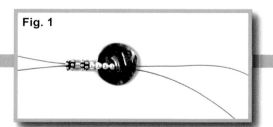

Fig. 1

Fig. 2

Dimensions
8 inches long

Materials
- 6 assorted double-shank connector buttons
- 1 single-shank button closure
- Spool of .014 beading wire
- 28 round stone beads, 6mm–turquoise
- 46 daisy spacer beads, 5mm– sterling silver
- 28 beads, 3mm–sterling silver
- 2 crimp beads–sterling silver

Additional Supplies
Basic beading supplies

For product information, see page 124.

Instructions

1. Holding two 15½-inch strands of beading wire together, string two daisy spacers, one crimp bead, and two spacers. Add four silver beads and pass through the button shank with both wires (**Fig. 1**).

2. Add four silver beads on the other side of the button shank and pass back through the two spacers, crimp bead, and two remaining spacers (**Fig. 2**).

3. Hold the tails of the wire and adjust the beads and button so there are no gaps. Crimp the crimp bead and trim excess wire (see Technique Guide, page 114).

4. Separate the two remaining strands of wire and string each wire with one silver bead.

5. To each wire add one daisy spacer, one turquoise stone, one daisy spacer, one turquoise stone, and one daisy spacer.

6. Pass the top wire through the top shank of a double-shank connector. Pass the bottom wire through the bottom shank of the connector (**Fig. 3**).

7. Repeat steps 5 and 6 using the remaining five double-shank connectors.

8. Add one daisy spacer and one silver bead to each wire.

9. Hold the two wire ends in one hand and the button closure end of the bracelet in the other hand. With the unfinished end at the top, carefully dangle the bracelet to allow the beads to settle in properly, eliminating gaps. Carefully lay down the bracelet.

10. Holding both wires, pass through two daisy spacers, one crimp bead, two daisy spacers, and 18 silver beads. Pass back through the two daisy spacers, crimp bead, and two daisy spacers (**Fig. 4**).

11. Hold the excess wire and make final adjustments to the tension. Crimp the crimp bead and trim excess wire.

Tools:

Crimping pliers

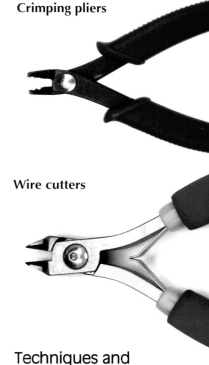

Wire cutters

Techniques and Skills Learned:
- Stringing
- Crimping

Notes

Fig. 3

Fig. 4

Christmastinis

Provided by Paula Radke Dichroic Beads

With a little wire wrapping, you can show off your style at the next holiday party with a chic martini set dripping in beads!

Inspiration

Martinis are such a sleek, sophisticated drink, and I wanted to reflect that in a martini set. Dichroic beads provide the perfect look, and the red, green, and silver create a festive holiday palette.

Materials

- Martini shaker of choice
- Martini glass of choice
- Assortment of dichroic beads—green, red, silver
- Assortment of dichroic spacer beads—green, red, silver
- Assortment of fire-polished beads—ruby, silver
- 2 packages 22-gauge wire—silver

Additional Supplies

Basic beading supplies

For product information, see page 124.

Instructions

Shaker

1. Cut 80 inches of wire. Starting at the top of the handle, place the end of the wire underneath the handle and hold down with your thumb. Wrap the wire around the handle a few times, securing the loose end on the bottom and using your thumb to keep the wire tight between wraps.

2. Add dichroic beads to cover the width of the handle. Wrap the wire around the handle once or twice to secure the beads. Place random shapes and sizes of dichroic beads in between fire-polished beads, and repeat until the handle is completely covered in beads.

3. To finish, slide the loose end under one of the wraps at the bottom of the handle and pull tight. Loop around again and pull tight with pliers. Repeat five to seven times. Trim excess wire.

4. If the shaker has a top, cut 10 inches of wire, place the end at the base of the top, and wrap to secure the end. String enough small dichroic spacer beads to go completely around the top once. Wrap with beaded wire, and continue to wrap tightly two more times.

5. To finish, feed the end of the wire through the beaded portion and pull tight with pliers; repeat two times and cut excess with cutters.

Martini Glass

1. Cut 80 inches of wire. Starting at the base, place the end of the wire on the stem and hold with your thumb. Wrap a few times around the stem to secure the loose end, using your thumb to keep the wire tight between wraps.

2. Randomly string dichroic and fire-polished beads to wrap one time around the stem. Wrap the beaded wire around the stem once or twice to secure the beads.

3. Repeat step 2 until beads have been wrapped all the way up the stem.

4. Finish in the same manner as step 5 of the shaker instructions.

Tools:

Flat nose pliers

Wire cutters

Techniques and Skills Learned:

- Wirework

Notes

Jade with a Twist Necklace

Designed by Lori Pate-Greene
for The Beadery

A summer necklace of
clear, crisp greens and
light gold accents is just the sort of
thing you want with a summer dress for a stroll in the
park or dinner on the patio. Basic wire working techniques add
a stylish and interesting accent to this fresh necklace.

Dimensions

19-inch necklace with a 2-inch pendant

Materials

- 2 packages specialty bead set—light jade
- 3 packages round and floral spacers, 3mm—gold-tone
- 1 package crimp beads—gold-tone
- 1 package "S" clasps—gold-tone
- 1 spool 20-gauge wire—gold-tone
- 1 head pin, 2 inches long—gold-tone
- 2 jump rings, ¼ inch–gold-tone
- Beading wire

Additional Supplies

Basic beading supplies

For product information, see page 124.

Instructions

Pendant

1. Cut two 6-inch pieces of 20-gauge wire. Insert both pieces of wire into one large twisted oval bead. Bend wires on each side so they cross over each other (**Figs. 1a** and **1b**).

2. Gently twist each pair of wires to secure (**Fig. 2**).

3. To create the wire spiral, form a loop at the wire end with the round nose pliers (see Technique Guide, page 114). Grasp the loop securely and continue bending the wire around the initial loop until the spiral is close to the oval twist bead. Repeat for the remaining three wire ends to complete the main pendant (**Fig. 3**).

4. On one side of the pendant, add one jump ring to each of the spiraled wires (**Fig. 4**). This side is now the top of the pendant.

5. Cut one 2½-inch piece of 20-gauge wire and bend it in half using the round nose pliers. Measure ¼ inch from bend, and fold over both wires (**Fig. 5**). Finish each end of the wire with a small spiral as in step 3.

6. Referring to **Fig. 6**, attach this wire piece to the bottom of the pendant (opposite the jump rings).

7. Stack a head pin with one green rondelle, one Baroque bead, and one 3mm round gold-tone bead. Make a loop at the top of the head pin (see Technique Guide, page 114) and attach to the bottom of the pendant before closing (**Fig. 7**).

Necklace

1. Cut one 25-inch piece of beading wire. Pass the end through a crimp bead, half of the "S" clasp, and back through the crimp bead. Crimp the crimp bead to secure.

2. String about 8¾ inches of beads onto the beading wire, following the pattern as shown in the photo or creating your own. String one jump ring holding the pendant, add one green rondelle, one 6mm round, and one green rondelle, and then add the second jump ring. Repeat the beading pattern to complete the second half of the necklace.

3. To complete the necklace, add a crimp bead and the remaining half of the "S" clasp as in step 1. Trim excess wire and tuck into the beads.

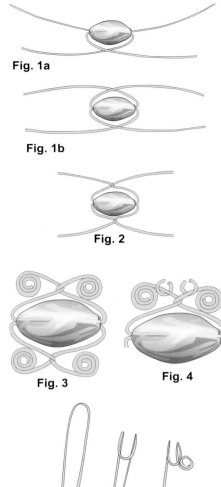

Fig. 1a

Fig. 1b

Fig. 2

Fig. 3

Fig. 4

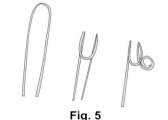

Fig. 5

Fig. 6

Fig. 7

Tools:

Chain nose pliers

Round nose pliers

Crimping pliers

Wire cutters

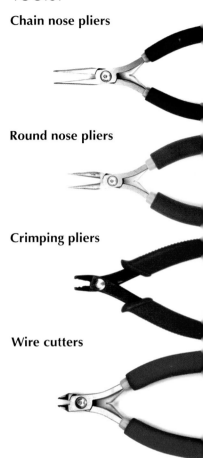

Ruler

No. R590-15 **WESTCOTT®**

Techniques and Skills Learned:

- Stringing
- Crimping
- Wirework:
  Creating wire spirals

Notes

Bohemian Mood Beading

Designed by Barbara Matthiessen

Make your own, one-of-a-kind beads using your favorite fabrics
or fabric scraps. Use your creations to embellish a wood frame and pillow
to add a modern, ethnic edge to your home décor.

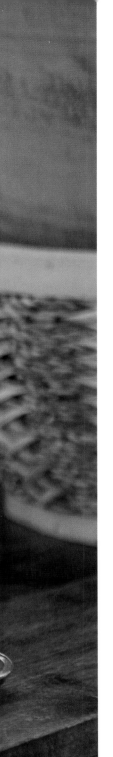

Inspiration

I adore fabrics of all kinds and wanted to incorporate more into my beadwork. I've made self-painted fabric and beads for a long time now, but wanted a different look and feel. I started experimenting with a variety of print fabrics until I found types that made beads with an ethnic appeal. Once I had a pile of fabric bead tubes, I started stacking beads and spacers around them, adding wires and more and more beads until I found some combinations that set my world on fire.

Dimensions

Frame: 8 inches square
Pillow: 18 inches x 11 inches

Tips

• Look for bright, strong contrast print fabrics. Stripes, geometrics, and ethnic prints are perfect as long as the scale is small. Mottled solids and border prints are great, too.
• When choosing where and how to cut your fabric, consider how much pattern will show when rolled up. Place stripes so they will roll around the skewer.
• Use one main color of E bead and pick a dominant metal to bring some continuity to your design.
• Mix it up! Don't be shy mixing "fancies" with "plain janes" or earthy beads.

Materials

Fabric tube beads
• 5 inch x 8 inch piece of fabric (one piece per tube)
• Fabric glue
• Crystal clear protective spray coating—matte
• Dimensional decoupage glue

Pillow
• 18-inch x 20-inch damask-style placemat
• 1 bead, 12mm—black/gold
• 62 petal spacer beads—silver
• 6 triangle beads—silver
• 1 tube of E beads—black
• 1 tube of E beads—rust and gold
• Variegated beads—tie dye

Frame
• 8-inch rounded edge square wood frame (with 3¼-inch opening)
• Photograph or fabric panel to fit opening
• Acrylic paint—licorice and honeycomb
• Antiquing medium—apple butter brown
• Crystal clear protective spray coating—matter
• 1 spool of 24-gauge wire—tinned copper
• Variety of fabric tube beads
• Variety of beads: silver, spacers, E beads, tie dye beads, small glass beads, and metal beads—colors to match

Additional Supplies

Basic beading supplies, clothespins, metal clothes hanger, paper towels, polyester fiberfill, sandpaper, sewing pins, water dish

For product information, see page 124.

 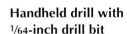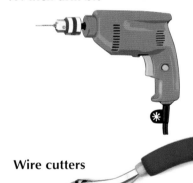

Instructions

Fabric tube beads

1. Cut or tear fabric to size. *Note:* Fabric needs to be 1 inch shorter than skewer length to clip to hanger to dry.

2. Place fabric wrong side up on work surface. Apply 1-inch-wide band of glue to one long side (**Fig. 1**).

3. Place skewer on the long side opposite the glue. Roll fabric up onto skewer (**Fig. 2**). Smooth glued edges down and around fabric roll (**Fig. 3**). Clip to hanger to dry.

4. Apply two coats of crystal clear coating to fabric tubes to prevent soiling. Follow manufacturer's instructions for application and drying time.

5. Slide beads off skewers. When ready to use, clip tubes to create beads the desired length. Dab dimensional decoupage glue on cut ends to prevent fraying and make them sturdier.

Pillow

Note: Refer to the bead medallion closeup.

1. Fold the placemat in half to find its exact center. Stitch the washer in the center using a doubled length of thread. Stitch from the backside, across the washer, and then to the backside in a couple of places. Stitch the black/gold bead in the center of the washer.

2. Place pins radiating out evenly from the center to guide bead placement. Remove pins as you work around the washer. Stitch 2½-inch "bead runs" at the north, south, east, and west positions. Backstitch through each bead to securely attach. (See Technique Guide, page 114).

North, south, east, and west bead runs: two E beads, one round tie dye bead, one E bead, one spacer, 1½-inch fabric bead, one spacer, three E beads. Add an additional spacer with an E bead center at the ends of the east and west bead runs.

3. Fill in between the north, south, east, and west bead runs with shorter runs of E beads, spacers, fabric beads, and silver triangle beads, referring to the photo for placement ideas. Continue filling in and adding bead run spokes as desired.

4. Fold the placemat in half lengthwise, wrong sides together, with ½ inch of overlap. Pin in a couple spots to hold in place. The bead medallion should be centered on the top side.

5. Stitch a 12-inch line of beads along each side edge of the pillow front using the woven edge pattern as a guide. Stitch a combination of E beads, tie dye beads, fabric beads (with spacers on each end), and triangle beads using a backstitch.

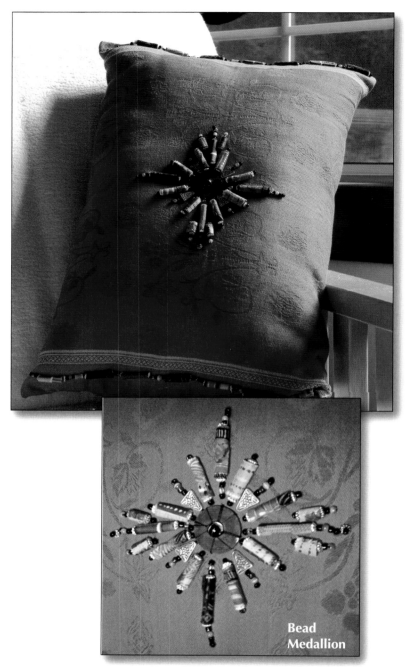

Bead Medallion

6. Slipstitch ends and back overlap using thread to match pillow. Leave a 5-inch opening in the back overlap. Stuff pillow with fiberfill. Finish stitching overlap closed.

Frame

1. Drill holes on all four sides of frame along inner and outer edges ½ inch apart and ¼ inch in (**Fig. 4**). Start the first side hole in a corner just past the curve. Drill two holes in each corner on the diagonal and ¼ inch in from edges. Sand any rough spots.

2. Paint the frame black and allow to dry. Dry brush brown paint in streaks across the frame and allow to dry. Sand frame to remove paint along edges and randomly across face. Wipe off sanding dust. Apply antiquing medium with a paintbrush, then wipe off with a paper towel. Allow to dry.

3. Apply two coats of crystal clear coating following the manufacturer's instructions for application and drying time.

4. Add beads to the frame starting with the corners. Cut 8-inch lengths of wire. Fold a loop in one end, then string on several beads of choice. Test the bead pattern length by holding it up to drilled holes; beads should end just before next hole. Insert the wire ends through two different drilled holes to backside. Twist wire ends together and trim the excess. Bend wire twists down against frame. Repeat same pattern in all four corners.

5. Repeat step 4 to bead the sides of the frame, creating six different bead patterns on each side. Use the same pattern in the same position on each side.

6. Insert photo or fabric panel into opening. *Note:* Depending on how photo or fabric is oriented, this frame is easily hung on the diagonal.

Be forewarned—this technique is *addictive* and a great way to use up bead and fabric odds and ends!

Fig. 1

Fig. 2

Fig. 3

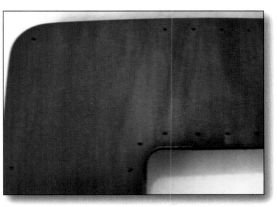

Fig. 4

Luxurious Links

Designed by Beth Spicker

Learn wire wrapping and linking secrets as you create each sparkling component of this bracelet.

Inspiration

I wanted the full, lavish look of a cha-cha bracelet to show off these crystals, but I didn't want a stretchy band that pinched my wrist. In my first few attempts to engineer a design, the beads would flop over, hiding the focal beads. With this link assembly, the large silver beads are always on top.

Tips

• Don't let the number of wrapped loops keep you from trying this bracelet. This is a great TV-time project. Make all of the wrapped loops while watching your favorite programs, and then sit down and assemble the bracelet later.

• Use good quality beads. The materials are what make this bracelet look so rich. I have tried using lesser quality beads, and it simply doesn't look as nice.

• Use silver beads with interesting granulation or texture to contrast with the smooth amethyst.
• It is the nature of sterling silver to tarnish. To maintain the beauty of your bracelet, keep it in an airtight bag when not being worn.
• Safety first! Even very small pieces of wire can do serious damage to your eyes. When you snip wire, cup your free hand over the top of the cutters to prevent the wire end from flying. Also, be careful not to get your fingers too close to the blades!

Variation

For a less chunky bracelet, consider scaling down this design. When purchasing materials, replace each bead with one that is one or two sizes smaller (i.e., where the instructions call for an 8mm crystal, purchase a 6mm or 7mm crystal instead). *Note:* 4mm beads are generally too small for this design unless stacked with other beads.

Dimensions
7 inches long

Materials
• 50 round crystals, 6mm—violet opal
• 26 bicone crystals, 6mm—crystal
• 13 fancy round crystals, 8mm—tanzanite
• 26 round beads, 6mm—dark amethyst
• 19 round beads, 8mm—dark amethyst
• 19 daisy spacers, 6mm—sterling silver
• 6 focal beads, 10mm x 8mm—sterling silver
• 12 round beads, 2mm—sterling silver
• 45 round beads, 3mm—sterling silver
• 140 22-gauge head pins, 1½ inches long—sterling silver
• 38 16-gauge open jump rings, 7⁄32-inch inside diameter—sterling silver
• 1-strand box clasp, 1½ inches (measured ring to ring)—sterling silver

Additional Supplies
Basic beading supplies

For product information, see page 124.

Tools:

Bent chain nose pliers

Flat nose pliers (2 pairs)

Flush cutters

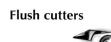

Round nose pliers

Techniques and Skills Learned:
• Wirework:
  Wire wrapping
  Working with jump rings

Notes

Instructions

Making bead components

1. Stack each bead (or bead set) listed below onto a head pin until beads and head pins have been used up:

* one 6mm violet opal round crystal;
* one 8mm tanzanite crystal;
* one 6mm round dark amethyst;
* one 3mm silver round bead + one 6mm crystal bicone;
* one 3mm silver round bead + one 6mm daisy spacer + one 8mm round dark amethyst;
* one 2mm silver round + one 10mm x 8mm sterling silver focal bead + one 2mm silver round.

2. Using round nose pliers, bent chain nose pliers, and flush cutters, make a wrapped loop at the top of each bead stack (see Technique Guide, page 114).

Assembling the bracelet

Note: The chain is built from the back and creates a pattern of two parallel vertical rings connected with one horizontal ring (see photo below).

1. Harden jump rings by working them back and forth several times with two pairs of flat nose pliers. Be careful not to distort the shape of the ring. Use a tearing (back and forth) motion to open rings—never pull them apart out to the left and right (see Technique Guide, page 114). Spread the open rings out on a flat surface. *Note:* If you are right-handed, leave jump rings open on the push away; if you are left-handed, leave open on the pull. This will make it easier to string beads onto the open ring and create the chain.

2. Separate clasp and lay decorative portion of clasp upside down with rings pointing right (left for lefties).

3. Refer to **Fig. 1** as you add bead components to jump rings. Pick up an open jump ring with bent chain nose pliers and string on *bead components* in this order to form Group A:

* 6mm violet opal round crystal
* 8mm tanzanite crystal
* 3mm silver round bead + 6mm crystal bicone
* 6mm round dark amethyst

4. Feed Group A jump ring up through ring of clasp.

5. Close jump ring securely using two pairs of pliers—**Do not leave any gap in the jump ring.**

6. Pick up another open jump ring and string on *bead components* in this order to form Group B:

* 6mm round dark amethyst
* 3mm silver round bead + 6mm daisy spacer + 8mm round dark amethyst
* 3mm silver round bead + 6mm crystal bicone
* 6mm violet opal round crystal

Note: Don't worry about counting how many components you make. Keep making bead components until you have used up all the bead quantities in the materials list.

7. Feed the Group B jump ring up through ring of clasp and close jump ring just like in step 4.

8. Refer to **Fig. 2** as you complete the following steps for the horizontal jump ring assembly. String one violet opal bead component (1) onto an open jump ring and feed through closed Group B jump ring from step 7 (the 6mm amethyst on the Group B ring should be closest to you).

9. String one sterling silver bead component (2) onto the open jump ring from step 8 and feed through closed Group A jump ring from step 4 (the violet opal crystal should be closest to you).

10. String another violet opal bead component (3) onto the open jump ring from step 9 and close jump ring.

11. String Group B bead components onto an open jump ring in the opposite direction as before (**Fig. 1**—flipped). Feed jump ring up through horizontal ring from step 10. Close jump ring.

12. String Group A bead components onto an open jump ring in the opposite direction as before (**Fig. 1**—flipped). Feed jump ring up through horizontal ring from step 10 in front of the Group B jump ring and close ring.

13. Referring to **Fig. 3**, string one violet opal bead component (1) onto another open jump ring. Working from back to front, feed through flipped Group B jump ring, string on one 8mm amethyst bead component (2), feed through flipped Group A jump ring, and then string on another violet opal bead component (3). Close jump ring. The jump ring pattern should now begin looking like the diagram in **Fig. 4**.

14. Continue building chain in this manner, alternating between the first Group A and B jump rings and the second (flipped) Group A and B components and following the horizontal jump ring instructions in steps 8-13 until all but the last eight bead components are used (one Group A and one Group B).

15. To attach second half of clasp, feed an open jump ring through ring on clasp. Continuing pattern of chain, string on last group of bead components, and then feed jump ring through last horizontal ring added. Close jump ring.

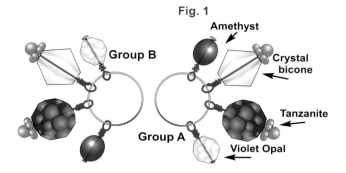

Fig. 1

Group B
Group A
Amethyst
Crystal bicone
Tanzanite
Violet Opal

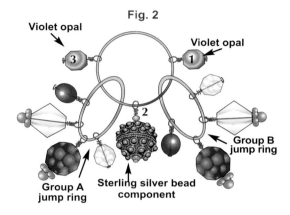

Fig. 2

Violet opal
Violet opal
Group B jump ring
Group A jump ring
Sterling silver bead component

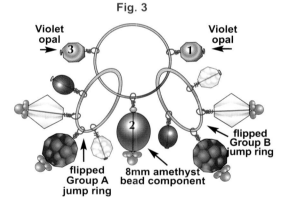

Fig. 3

Violet opal
Violet opal
flipped Group B jump ring
flipped Group A jump ring
8mm amethyst bead component

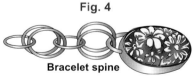

Fig. 4

Bracelet spine

Forget-Me-Not Necklace & Brooch

Designed by Lori Pate-Greene for The Beadery

Create these flowery, yet stunning accessories with few twists of *bead-embellished* wire and a little wire shaping.

Tips

• Finished brooch may be as delicate or full of beads as desired.
• When twisting 28-gauge wire, do not over twist; just twist enough until the bead is held in place.
• To add more wire, thread a new piece around the center of a cluster and twist the wire together to secure. Continue beading.

Dimensions

Necklace: 17 inches
Brooch: 2½ inches x 1½ inches

Necklace Materials

• 1 package of lobster claw clasps—gold-tone
• 3 packages of glass flower beads—blue
• 2 packages of pressed beads—green foil
• 2 packages of miniature glass lampwork beads—green
• 1 spool of 28-gauge wire—gold-tone
• 1 package of round beads, 3mm and 4mm—gold-tone
• 1 package of small jump rings—gold-tone
• 1 package of double cup fold over bead tips—gold-tone

Brooch Materials

• 1 package of glass flower beads—blue
• 1 package of pressed beads—green foil
• 1 package of spacer beads—aqua
• 1 package of round beads with floral rondelles, 3mm—gold-tone
• 1 spool of 20-gauge wire—gold-tone
• 1 spool of 28-gauge wire—gold-tone
• 1 package of pin backs with holes—gold tone

Additional Supplies

Basic beading supplies, foam core board, pins

For product information, see page 124.

Tools:

Flat nose pliers

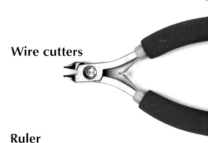

Round nose pliers

Wire cutters

Ruler

No. R590-15 **WESTCOTT®**

Techniques and Skills Learned:

• Wirework:
  Embellished wire wrapping
  Working with jump rings
  Wire twisting
  Creating wire spirals

Notes

Necklace Instructions

1. Cut two 48-inch pieces of 28-gauge wire and bend each piece in half. Place the bent end of one wire into a double cup fold over bead tip, and close bead tip with flat nose pliers. Twist ½ inch of the wire ends together to create the main twisted strand. Repeat this step with the second piece of wire.

2. Add jump rings to both double cup fold over bead tips using the round nose pliers. Add a lobster claw to one jump ring.

3. Clasp ends together and attach necklace to foam core board work surface using pins. *Note:* Work both sides of the necklace at the same time, creating a symmetrical look.

4. Slide one fancy lampwork bead up one wire to the end of the main twisted strand. Twist the two wires together, adding about ¼ inch to the main twisted strand (**Fig. 1**). Repeat on the opposite side.

5. *Branched leaf.* Add one foil pressed bead to each wire, leave ¼ inch of slack space, and bend wire back against the bead (**Fig. 2**). *Note:* Do not go back through the bead with the wire. Twist slack wire together. Repeat on the opposite side.

6. Twist the two wires together, adding about ½ inch to the main twisted strand. Continue adding foil pressed beads and fancy lampwork beads as described in steps 4 and 5 for about 4½ inches on each side. *Note:* On some branched leaves, create three leaves instead of two.

7. *Three-flower cluster.* Immediately after the last set of branched leaves, thread one flower bead and one 3mm gold round bead. Pass back through the flower, which will anchor it to the wire. Repeat with the second wire. Add one more flower and 3mm gold bead combination using the outside wire (**Fig. 3**). Twist both wires together about ¼ inch to add to the main twisted strand. Repeat on the opposite side.

8. Create a branched leaf after the flower cluster on each side as described in step 5.

9. Twist two wires together, creating another ½ inch of the main twisted strand. Cut off untwisted wire. With round nose pliers, twist and tuck wire ends around one of the flowers in the cluster to secure. Repeat on the opposite side.

10. *Adding more wire.* Cut two more 48-inch pieces of wire and bend each in half. Slip the bent wire behind the flower cluster, taking care to anchor new wire in existing wire. Twist both wires together for 1 inch, which will secure the new wire and create more of the main twisted strand. Repeat on the opposite side.

11. Add ¾ inch of assorted beads (small lampwork, 4mm gold, etc.) to the 1-inch area of the main twisted strand from step 10. Repeat the three-flower cluster described in step 7. Repeat on the opposite side.

12. On one wire, thread one bell flower and one 4mm gold bead. Repeat two more times. Leave ¼ inch of slack wire between the flowers and the main twisted strand. Skip the bottom 4mm gold bead and pass wire back through remaining beads (**Fig. 4**). Twist slack wire to tighten. Repeat on opposite side.

13. Around the cluster of three flowers, use the branch leaf technique from step 5 to add pressed foil beads, lampwork beads, and 4mm gold beads. Vary the length of twisted wire as desired. Anchor each branched leaf behind a three-flower cluster. Repeat five to seven times to create a floral spray. Refer to photo as a guide for placement. Repeat on the opposite side.

14. Using both wires, create 1½ inches of main twisted strand on each side. Snip off one wire from the left side of the necklace. Snip off one wire from the right side of the necklace. Thread on an assortment of beads (pressed foil beads, lampwork beads, and 4mm gold beads). Select one fancy lampwork bead as the central connection. Thread left-side wire through fancy lampwork bead, and create a three-flower cluster as in step 7. Then thread the right-side wire through the same fancy lampwork bead in the opposite direction and make another three-flower cluster.

15. Create a central floral spray using the techniques in steps 12 and 13. When desired fullness has been achieved, end by twisting the two wires together about ½ inch. Snip the loose excess wire. With round nose pliers, twist and tuck wire ends behind floral spray.

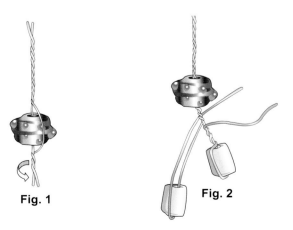

Fig. 1   **Fig. 2**

Brooch Instructions

1. Cut one 8-inch and one 6-inch piece of 20-gauge wire.

2. *Spiral Ends.* Form a loop on each end of each wire piece with the round nose pliers (see Technique Guide, page 114). On the shorter wire, make two 2½-inch-diameter spirals; on the longer wire, make one 2½-inch-diameter spiral and one 1½-inch-diameter spiral, oriented as shown in **Fig. 5**.

3. Cut one 24-inch piece of 28-gauge wire. Wrap 28-gauge wire around the two spiral pieces to secure as shown in **Fig. 5**.

4. Attach spirals to pin back by threading wire through holes of pin back and wrapping wire around spiraled wires and pin back.

5. *Attaching flower cluster.* Create a central cluster of flowers (approximately four to seven flowers and/or beads) to help hide pin back. Secure flowers with a 3mm gold bead and wire (**Fig. 6**). Anchor wire each time new beads are added by sliding it through any holes in the pin back or sliding through the wire-wrapped area.

6. *Twisted wire with bead.* Vary both beads (foil pressed beads, 3mm gold beads, small beads from aqua mix) and the lengths of wire as desired. Thread wire through bead or beads, bend it back against the bead, and twist (holding the bead) to secure (**Fig. 7**). *Note:* Always anchor the wire strand to pin back or slide through wire-wrapped area before adding another twisted wire and bead.

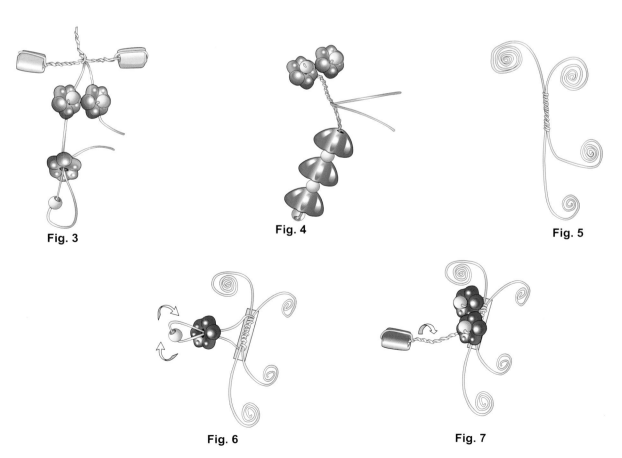

Fig. 3

Fig. 4

Fig. 5

Fig. 6

Fig. 7

"Lucies" Garden Bracelet

Designed by Kelli Burns

Embellish a plain strand of beads with seed bead and Lucite flower fringe to create a colorful flower garden bracelet. This lightweight project is packed with bright beads in a variety of shapes and colors.

Tips

• If you add crystals to your design, double the thread and pass through each crystal multiple times.

• Always check for loose fringe and thread pieces and carefully trim them. The bracelet should look like a garden of flowers with no visible thread ends.

Dimensions

7½ inches long

Materials

- 1g to 2g of size 6/0 seed beads—coordinating color
- 1g to 3g of size 8/0 seed beads—coordinating color
- 2g to 4g of size 11/0 seed beads—coordinating color
- 3g to 4g Miyuki Delica size 11/0 cylinder beads—coordinating color
- Focal lampwork bead (or several smaller lampwork beads) of choice
- 10 to 30 Lucite flowers and leaves—assorted colors and sizes
- Assorted filler beads, 4mm or smaller—coordinating colors
- Clasp of choice
- .014 or .019 beading wire (.014 allows you to sew through the bracelet more times; use .019 if the focal bead has sharp edges)
- 2 crimp tubes—sterling silver

Additional Supplies

Basic beading supplies, bead design board, bead stopper, beeswax

For product information, see page 124.

Instructions

1. *Making the base wire.* Lay out the size 6/0 seed beads and focal bead(s) on the bead design board. Cut a length of beading wire to desired bracelet length plus 1 inch for crimping. String a crimp tube, a seed bead, half the clasp, and pass back through the seed bead and crimp tube. Crimp the crimp tube. String the seed beads and focal bead(s) onto the wire to the desired length.

2. Crimp the second end as described in step 1, checking the sizing on your wrist. *Note:* Leave a little room (the width of one or two seed beads) between the last seed bead and the second crimp bead for sewing (**Fig. 1**).

3. Cut an 18-inch piece of thread, condition it, and attach to the base wire after the first seed bead with an overhand half-hitch knot (see Technique Guide, page 114). Pass through the base second seed and add three size 11/0 seeds and one size 8/0 seed (stop bead). Skip the size 8/0 seed and pass back through the remaining seeds to bracelet base, pulling snugly to create the first fringe (**Fig. 2**). Make two more fringes in the same manner, adding additional size 11/0 seeds to vary the fringe lengths. *Note:* After every few fringes, knot the thread to the base wire with a half-hitch knot. If one piece of fringe breaks, you'll lose only those fringe beads and your bracelet will still be intact.

4. Pass through the third base seed and make two to three more fringes of varying lengths and seed bead combinations. Work down the bracelet, adding fringes to achieve desired fullness. When you reach the end of a piece of thread, knot it on the base wire and start another length. For additional fullness, string Delica "vines" or loops along the base wire.

5. To add Lucite and other filler beads to the bracelet, make fringe as described in step 3, adding beads of choice as you work and using a small seed as a stop bead. For a more interesting bracelet, string some Lucite beads close to the base wire and add some on the ends of longer fringes (**Fig. 3**). *Note:* Adding leaves to longer fringes looks especially neat, as if the leaves are growing on vines.

half-hitch knot

Fig. 1

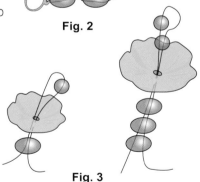

Fig. 2

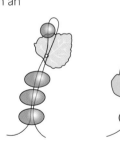

Fig. 3

Tools:

Beading needle and size D nylon beading thread

Chain nose pliers

Crimping pliers

Wire cutters

Beading scissors

Techniques and Skills Learned:

- Stringing
- Crimping
- Bead embellishment:
  Bead stacks
  Fringe

Notes

Beaded Eyeglass Cases

Designed by Linda Wyszynski

With a needle, thread, and some simple surface embellishment, you can turn a few plain pieces of fabric into a bright and functional accessory.

General Instructions

1. Tie a knot in the end of the thread to begin stitching. For surface beading, secure the thread on the back of the fabric using a looped knot (**Fig. 1**). When you reach the end of a beaded area, tie the thread on the back of the fabric with two knots.

2. If you run out of thread while working the edging of a case, start a new thread through several previous beads, secure with a half hitch-knot, and continue out the working bead to continue (see Technique Guide, page 114).

3. When traveling with the thread on cases that use interfacing, run the thread between the interfacing and the felt. End the thread if it is necessary to travel more than 1 inch across the fabric.

4. When attaching a single bead or group of beads, pass through the fabric from back to front, slide the beads into place, then pass back through the fabric so the beads lie flat. Pass through larger beads and bead groups twice.

5. When attaching a line of single beads as in the paisley case, pass through the first and last bead twice to secure.

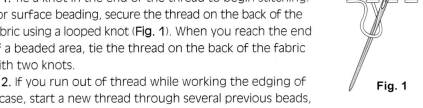

Fig. 1

Dimensions
3½ x 7 inches each

Paisley Case Materials
• 9-inch-square piece of fusible interfacing
• 9-inch-square piece, one in each color, of wool felt—orange spice and cardinal red
• 40 to 55 wood beads, 4mm—natural
• 45 to 50 wood tube beads, 3mm x 6mm—black
• 7 to 10 wood tube beads, 6mm x 9mm—light brown
• 1 tube size 11/0 seed beads—bone
• 9-inch-square piece of lining fabric—coordinating color

Black and White Case Materials
• 7-inch-square piece of ultra microfiber suede fabric—black
• ¼-inch-wide quilter's tape
• 1 tube Miyuki Delica crystals—white luster-lined
• 1 tube ToHo size 11/0 seed beads—white opaque luster
• 1 tube Matsuno size 11/0 seed beads—silky white
• 1 tube size 10/0 seed beads—pearl
• 1 strand 123-cut crystals—white-lined
• 12 bicone crystals, 4mm—white opal
• 15 bicone crystals, 4mm—white alabaster
• 12 star shine beads, 4mm—white opal
• 21 pearls, 4mm—cream
• 1 tube bugles—white, No. 3
• 5 mother-of-pearl leaves
• 9-inch-square piece of lining fabric—coordinating color

Additional Supplies
Basic beading supplies, iron, pencil or permanent black fine marker, tissue or tracing paper, tweezers

For product information, see page 124.

For product information, see page 124.

Beginner / Intermediate Project

Tools:

Beading needle and size A nylon beading thread

Sewing needle and thread

Beading scissors

Techniques and Skills Learned:
• Sewing:
    Blanket stitch
• Bead embroidery:
    Couching
    Picot stitch
    Scalloped stitch
    Single bead picot stitch

Notes

Paisley Case Instructions

Note: Use a double strand of orange nylon beading thread to attach all beads to this case.

Creating the case

1. Cut a 6¾-inch-square piece of fusible interfacing and a 7-inch-square piece of orange spice felt. Following the manufacturer's instructions, fuse the interfacing to the back of the felt.

2. Trace the paisley pattern (page 105) onto tissue paper and cut the shapes out of the cardinal red felt.

Embellishing the case

1. Referring to the photo for correct placement, attach each paisley by placing small stitches in several places along each edge with matching thread. Attach 4mm natural wood beads along the edge of each paisley and black wood tube beads along each outside edge. *Note:* Allow a small amount of orange felt to show between the tube beads and the edge of each paisley. Attach single light brown wood tube beads to the case as shown on the pattern.

Paisley Case

2. Along the top of a 6¾-inch-square piece of lining fabric, fold ⅛-inch over to the wrong side and iron in place. Stitch the lining to the inside of the case using matching thread, making sure the thread does not show on the front of the case.

3. Fold the felt in half and pin the edges together. Beginning at the bottom left, create a picot stitch edging using bone seed beads (**Fig. 2**). Continue along the right side of the case.

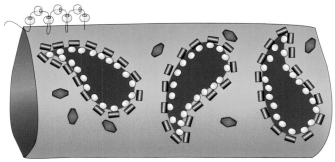

Fig. 2   *Note:* Beads are enlarged for emphasis.

Black and White Suede Fabric Case Instructions

Note: When couching beads, push the beads close together and take the needle straight down into the fabric in front of the previous bead to keep the rows straight. Pull the thread taut, but keep the fabric smooth.

Creating the case

1. Fold a 7-inch-square piece of tissue paper in half evenly. Open it up and center the right side of the paper over the black and white pattern on page 105 (**Fig. 3**). Trace the pattern and place the tissue paper on the front side of a 7-inch-square piece of suede fabric. *Note:* Do not use pins in the suede fabric! Instead, use quilter's tape to hold the pattern in place.

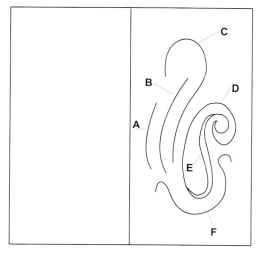

Fig. 3

2. Baste the pattern through the tissue paper onto the fabric with white sewing thread. *Note:* Be sure the basting thread shows on the back. Carefully remove the tissue paper and use tweezers to remove any remaining paper from under the stitches.

Embellishing the case

Note: Refer to **Fig. 3** as you work.

1. Couch white luster-lined crystal Delicas along Area A.

2. Couch alternating white opaque luster ToHo seeds and silky white Matsuno seeds along Area B.

3. Couch a size 10/0 pearl seed, a 4mm white opal bicone crystal, a size 10/0 pearl seed, and a 4mm white opal star shine bead along Area C. Repeat this pattern to the end of the section, ending with a size 10/0 pearl seed. Attach two mother-of-pearl leaves to the tip of the curve.

4. To create the "spikes" along Area C, couch a size 10/0 pearl seed, a white bugle, and a size 10/0 pearl seed in a line coming out from the second pearl seed above the mother-of-pearl leaves. Couch a spike coming out from each size 10/0 pearl seed

along Area C, alternating sides of the bead row, until you have placed five spikes on each side.

5. Couch size 11/0 white opaque luster ToHo seeds along Area D. Couch a row of 4mm white alabaster bicones in the center of Area D.

6. Couch the 123-cut white-lined crystals along Area E. Couch a single row of these crystals between Areas D and E.

7. Couch alternating size 10/0 pearl seeds and 4mm cream pearls along Area F. Attach a mother-of-pearl leaf at each curved end and one in the center of the bottom curve.

8. Along the top of a 6¾-inch-square piece of lining fabric, fold ⅛-inch over to the wrong side and iron in place. Stitch the lining to the inside of the case using matching thread, making sure the thread does not show on the front of the case.

9. Fold the felt in half evenly and use quilter's tape to hold the case together. Beginning on the bottom left of the case, create a basic beaded scallop stitch edging using size 11/0 white opaque luster ToHo seeds and two strands of black nylon beading thread (**Fig. 4**). *Note:* The seeds touching the fabric along the edge of the case are the "anchor beads." Pass through the fabric from back to front, add seven seeds, and pass back through the fabric, leaving the width of about four seeds between anchor beads. Pass back through the seventh seed, add six seeds, and pass back through the fabric, leaving the same amount of space between anchor beads. Continue this beading pattern along the bottom edge and along the right side of the case.

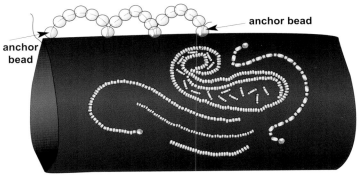

anchor bead

anchor bead

Fig. 4

Wine Bottle Cape

Designed by Merit Cape

Learn basic bead netting and fringe techniques while making a sparkling, festive drape for your favorite bottle of wine.

Tips

• Hang beads no more than 2 inches down the neck so the bottle can be held (and poured) comfortably.
• If you like, create an extended beaded chain to help keep beads in place while pouring wine.

Materials

• 18 size 4 pearls—silver and gray
• 42 size 4 glass beads—red and black
• 6 size 6 crystals—red
• 6 donut beads—red
• 12 glass leaf and grape charms—red and gold
• 2 tubes (one in each color) of size 11/0 seed beads—red and gold

Additional Supplies

Basic beading supplies

For product information, see page 124

Inspiration

I love to bead on glass bottles of all sorts, mostly because I love how the light on glass complements the glimmer of beads.

Tools:

Size 10 beading needle and size D nylon beading thread

Beading scissors

Techniques and Skills Learned:
- Bead weaving:
  Netting
  Fringe

Notes

Instructions

1. Using a 6-foot piece of nylon beading thread and referring to **Fig. 1** for the pattern, string 11 seed beads and a glass bead. Repeat this pattern five times. Pass through the first 12 beads again, making a circle and exiting from the first glass bead. Pass the short end of the string through the beads in the opposite direction to hide it.

2. Add eight seed beads, a pearl, and eight seeds. Pass through the second glass bead in line to make a loop hanging from the original circle (**Fig. 2**).

3. Repeat step 2 five more times. Always pass through the next glass bead in line to make loops around the circle. When making the last loop, pass through the last glass bead and down into seed beads of the original loop made, exiting the pearl on that loop (**Fig. 3**).

4. Add nine seeds, a glass bead, and nine seeds. Pass through the pearl on the following loop (**Fig. 4**). Continue with this new loop pattern, always taking the needle through the pearl on the next loop in line. When making the last loop, pass through the pearl on the original loop row made and then down through the seed beads of second loop row, exiting the glass bead on the second loop row (**Fig. 5**).

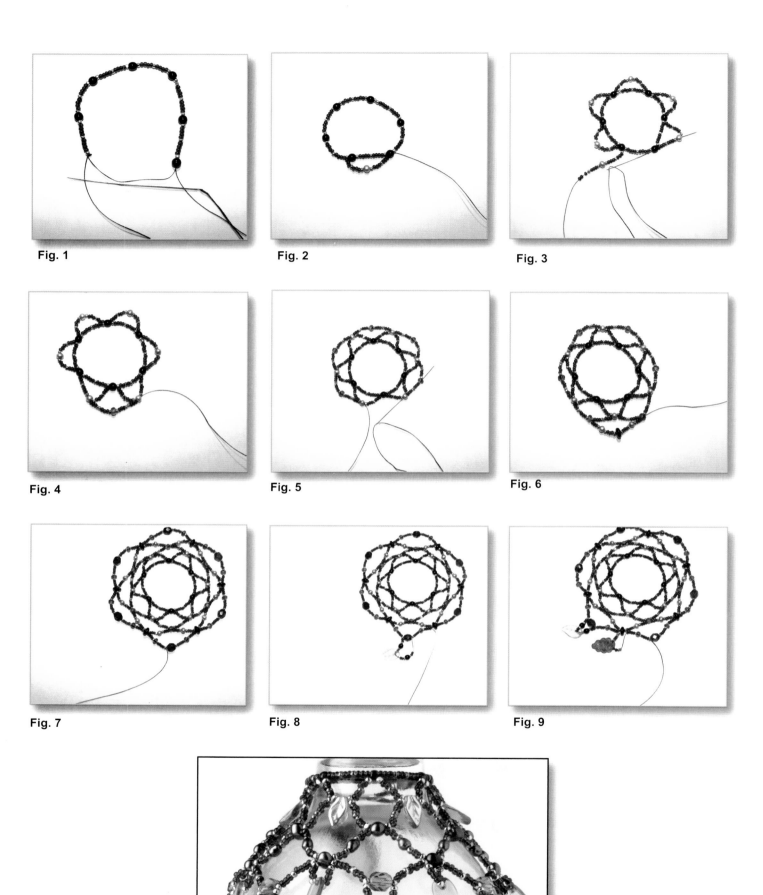

Fig. 1

Fig. 2

Fig. 3

Fig. 4

Fig. 5

Fig. 6

Fig. 7

Fig. 8

Fig. 9

5. String four seeds, a pearl, four seeds, and a donut bead. Continue stringing four seeds, a pearl, and another four seeds. Pass through the glass bead on the row above as you did on the last set of loops (**Fig. 6**). Repeat this pattern all the way around, exiting through the first donut bead.

6. String five seeds, a glass bead, five seeds, a crystal, five seeds, a glass bead, and five seeds. Pass through the donut bead in the previous row. Repeat this pattern all the way around, exiting just *before* the first crystal (**Fig. 7**).

7. Add three seeds, a glass bead, three seeds, a leaf charm, three seeds, a glass bead, and three seeds. Pass through the seeds on the opposite side of the crystal, exiting just before the next donut bead (**Fig. 8**).

8. Add five seeds, a grape charm, and five seeds. Pass through the seeds on the opposite side of the donut bead, exiting just before the next crystal (**Fig. 9**).

9. Continue alternating steps 7 and 8 all the way around. *Note*: The alternate ending may be used at this point. At the last focal bead on upper loop row, pass through focal bead and all beads following on that loop. To finish, make a half-hitch knot, pass through beads to hide excess string, and pull knot in.

Alternate ending: Extended Bead Chain: Pass through the last donut on the upper row, and then pass through seed beads just before the next crystal. String about 6½ inches of seeds, add a leaf bead or some other focal bead, and add four more seeds. Skip the last four beads, leaf bead, and next four beads and pass through the remainder of the seed bead chain. Knot the thread with a half-hitch knot and pass through the chain to hide excess.

Combine basic stringing with a little braiding know-how to create this bright bracelet!

Braided Cube Bracelet

Designed by Lou Musante

Inspiration

Constantly exposed to my wife's obsession with beads and jewelry making, I experimented with Japanese cord braiding. This bracelet is the result of my taking that experiment and combining it with cube beads to create a beaded bracelet.

Tip

The length of the braided section is determined by your desired overall length. The additional beads and clasp add approximately 1½ inches to the bracelet length, so plan the braided length accordingly.

Dimensions

7½-inch-long bracelet

Materials

- 36 inches of .014 stringing cord
- 1 clasp of choice
- 2 crimp tubes
- 1 round crimp bead
- 250 Japanese cube beads—assorted colors

Additional Supplies

Basic beading supplies, clear tape, small vise (or small squeeze clamp)

For product information, see page 124.

Instructions

1. Cut the stringing cord into three 12-inch lengths. Fold a piece of tape around each cord about 1½ - 2 inches from the end to act as a bead stop (**Fig. 1**). Add 7½ inches of cube beads on each cord. After stringing the beads, fold another piece of tape around the opposite end of each cord to retain beads (**Fig. 2**).

2. To attach the clasp, thread all three cords through three cube beads, one crimp tube, one end of the clasp, and back through the crimp tube (**Fig. 3**). Pull cords tight around clasp, slide crimp tube within about 1/16 inch of clasp, and squeeze with the crimping pliers (see Technique Guide, page 114). Use the wire cutters to cut off the excess wire and tuck ends into the first few beads. Remove the tape squares from the completed end of the bracelet.

3. Anchor the completed bracelet end from step 2 in the vise or squeeze clamp (**Fig. 4**). Beginning with one strand, slide the tape from the opposite end up the strand to eliminate all excess space between beads. Secure tape at this point. Repeat for each wire.

4. Begin basic three-strand braiding and continue until approximately 6 inches of beads are braided. After you've created 6 inches of braiding, check to see if the three cords have extra beads. Note the number of beads that need to be removed if necessary, then unbraid the bracelet and remove the extra beads. Replace the tape, take up the slack, and re-braid the bracelet. *Note: This is much easier than removing beads while trying to maintain the braiding tension.*

5. After braiding is complete, thread the three cords through the round crimp bead and slide the crimp tight against the beads. When all slack has been eliminated, crimp with the crimping pliers (**Fig. 5**). *Note: This extra crimp maintains the braid's tension while adding the remaining three beads and clasp.*

6. String three cube beads onto all three cords as in step 2. Add the crimp tube and pass the three cords around the clasp end and back through the crimp tube (**Fig. 6**). Pull the wires tight against the clasp and crimp the crimp tube.

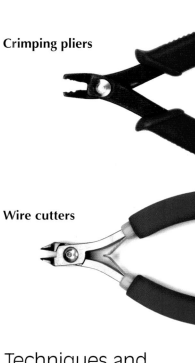

Fig. 1

Fig. 2

Fig. 3

Fig. 4

Fig. 5

Fig. 6

Beads to Go!

Designed by Katie Hacker for Beadalon

Learn what you'll need to assemble a Beads to Go! kit and how a simple "bead soup" can help you push past your creative boundaries!

Inspiration

The eclectic look of this multicolored bracelet was inspired by the artisan-style jewelry that I've seen in so many fashion magazines and catalogs. The colorful mixture of beads provides a dramatic backdrop for the unusual center bead.

Tip

You've probably heard the term "bead soup" before. But what is it? "Bead soup" refers to a random collection of various beads. I keep a tin on my desk where I stash any leftover beads that are too few to make it worth organizing them. From time to time, I scoop out a baggie-ful and put them in my travel beading kit. Using the soup is an exercise in creativity because it forces me to consider different color and texture combinations than the ones I normally use. Just like real soup, you don't have to make yours from scratch. Mixed packages of beads are widely available.

Dimensions

Vary

Materials

- Rectangular bead with leaf impression—pewter
- 25-30 beads of choice ("bead soup")
- 1 spool of flexible beading wire—silver
- 2 head pins—silver
- 2 lever back ear wires—silver
- 2 crimp tubes—silver
- Toggle clasp—silver

For product information, see page 124.

Instructions

Basic bracelet to go

1. Measure your wrist. Leaving the beading wire attached to the spool, string on beads (including your focal bead) to fill a wire length 1 inch longer than your wrist size.

2. String a crimp tube and half of the clasp onto the wire end. Pass the wire end back through the crimp tube to form a small loop. Use a crimping tool to crimp it (see Technique Guide, page 114).

3. Leave 1 inch extra and cut the wire off the spool. Use a crimp tube to attach the second half of the clasp to the end of the bracelet. Cut off the extra wire or tuck it inside the last bead.

Basic earrings to go

String a small bead, a metal bead, and a small bead onto an eye pin. Make a loop above the top bead and attach it to an earring finding (see Technique Guide, page 114). String a medium-sized glass bead onto a head pin. Make a loop and attach it below the metal bead.

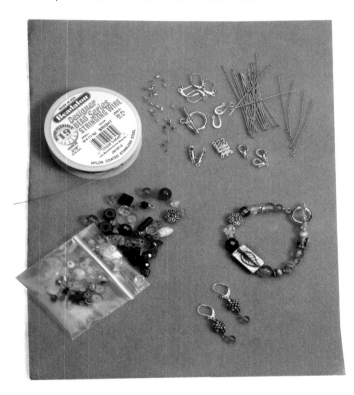

Tools:

Round nose pliers

Chain nose pliers

Crimping pliers

Wire cutters

Techniques and Skills Learned:

- Stringing
- Crimping
- Experimenting with color and texture

Notes

Make your own Beads to Go! *kit*

The materials list details exactly what you need to make Katie's Beads to Go! bracelet and earrings. Use her idea, concoct some bead soup from your existing bead stash, and put together your own unique Beads to Go! kit following the list below. Take this kit on your next weekend getaway or vacation and give your creativity a workout!

- Interesting focal beads • Small baggie of bead soup
- Selection of earring findings, clasps, head pins, and eye pins
- Spool of flexible beading wire • Crimp beads/tubes assortment
- Beading mat • Round nose pliers • Chain nose pliers • Wire cutters
- Crimping tool • Baggie or container of choice for storage

Glossary

Project Skill Levels
Beginner: Basic knowledge of some tools, materials, and beads. Not yet proficient in this type of work.
Intermediate: Working knowledge of basic techniques, tools, and materials needed to complete that particular project. Ready to learn new techniques and encounter some challenges.
Advanced: Experienced in the technique or medium being used. Ready for a challenge and looking to push beyond existing skills.

Basic Beading Supplies (BBS)
Basic beading supplies, used in most projects, include: a bead dish, beading tray or cloth work surface, beading needles, beading thread, thread conditioner, and scissors.

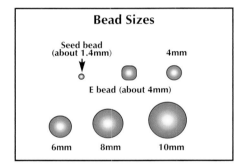

Bead Sizes
Seed bead (about 1.4mm)
4mm
E bead (about 4mm)
6mm   8mm   10mm

Measurement Converter

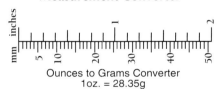

Ounces to Grams Converter
1oz. = 28.35g

Common Jewelry Measurements
Choker: 16 in.
Princess length necklace: 18 in.
Matinee length necklace: 24 in.
Opera length necklace: 32 in.
Rope or lariat: 48 in.
Bracelet: 7 in.
Anklet: 9 in.

Bead Count
Beads are commonly sold in 16-in. strands. Use this list to better calculate bead amounts on any given strand. List is based on a 400mm strand divided by the bead size:

2mm	203	3mm	136
4mm	100	6mm	67
8mm	50	10mm	41

Seed beads

Bugle beads

Faceted beads

Furnace glass beads

Crystal beads

Briolettes

Rondelles

Popular assorted shapes

Other common shapes

Assorted unusual shapes

Pearls

Focal beads

Lampwork beads

Metal beads

Sterling/Bali silver beads

Spacer beads

Findings

Findings are components, often made of metal, that are used to create the structure in a piece of jewelry. Clasps, charms, jump rings, head pins, and ear wires are all examples of findings.

Clasps

Lobster clasp

Toggle clasp

Hook and eye clasp

Box clasp

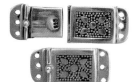

Slide lock clasp

S-clasp

Snap clasp

Spring ring clasp

Barrel clasp

Earring Findings

Ear posts

Lever back ear wires

French ear wires (fish hook)

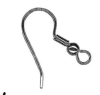

Other Findings

Crimp beads   **Crimp tubes**

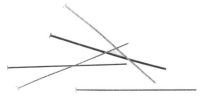

Head pins

Jump rings

Charms

Bead caps

9

8

7

6

5

4

3

2

1

0

Spacer bars

Cones

Bead tips

Tools & Supplies

Chain nose pliers

Pliers' jaws are flat on the inside and rounded on the outside. The flat surface creates right angle bends in wire. The rounded outside makes rounded bends. Their tapered point allows you to work in tight places. Pliers' tips look like this: ⊓ D

Crimp pliers

These specialty pliers have two grooves machined into the jaws and are made to crush and close (fold over) crimp beads/tubes.

Flush cutters

The cutting jaws are angled for an accurate cut.

Nylon jaw pliers

These pliers are used to smooth wire out before use. Lightly grip the wire with the nylon jaws and pull it through.

Round nose pliers

The name refers to the shape of the pliers' jaws. Use round nose pliers to create loops and curves in wire. Most round nose pliers' jaws taper to a point, allowing you to vary the size of your loops and bends. Plier tips look like this: OO

Flat nose pliers

The jaws of flat nose pliers are smooth and can be used to grip, bend, and flatten wire without marking it.

Beading scissors

A pair sharp, fine-pointed beading scissors is a necessary tool if you're working with beading thread. Their sharp blades make a precise cut and will help prevent the thread from fraying.

Beading needles

The sizes of needles are indicated by number; the most commonly used beading needle sizes are #10 and #12. *Note:* Beading needles differ from ordinary sewing needles because the eye is narrower to allow passage through a bead. The higher the number, the smaller the needle's diameter.

Needle threader

A needle threader helps push thread through the small eye of a beading needle with minimal effort and eye strain.

Glue

Glue is often used to give extra strength and security to knots in beading thread. Cyanoacrylate glue is used to bond metal parts together (such as a memory wire end cap to the end of a piece of memory wire) in a jewelry piece.

Tweezers

Beading tweezers are great to have on-hand to aid in knotting techniques or when you need to pick up and sort tiny beads.

WigJig tool

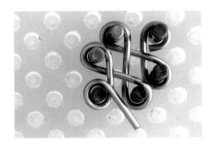

A WigJig tool creates and allows for consistent shape and form of wire designs. It consists of a base with movable pegs placed over a design template. Wire is then wrapped around the pegs as indicated on the design for a precise look.

Wire gauge wheel

This handy tool is used to accurately determine the thickness (gauge) of a piece of wire.

Wire end rounder with burr cup

Place the burr cup over the cut end of a piece of wire and twist the tool to smooth and round the edge.

Metal file

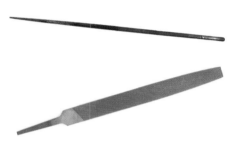

Use this tool to file the ends of your wires after cutting them to eliminate rough edges and exhibit good workmanship and attention to detail.

Chasing Hammer

Striking wire with the smooth face of the hammer will compress the wire, causing it to harden. The resulting flat wire creates an interesting look in projects. Also, hardening the wire will strengthen the clasp or a curve in an earring finding.

Hammer block

Place under the wire when flattening to serve as a solid surface and protect your work area.

Bead reamer

Use a bead reamer to enlarge, straighten, or complete the hole in a bead or pearl.

Millimeter gauge

A millimeter gauge will help you accurately measure all of your bead components.

Bead mat

A bead mat helps prevent beads from rolling off your work surface and provides a comfortable cushion for your hands while working.

Bead scoop

A bead scoop provides an efficient way to gather and organize your beads without using your hands.

Bead design board

A design board allows you to plan out jewelry designs before you begin stringing. It also keeps your beads organized in one place on your work surface.

Bead storage

Keep your beads safely stored in compartmentalized bead boxes or in containers with lids so they're easily accessible when you start creating!

Stringing Material

Flexible beading wire

Flexible beading wire is made of a bundle of stainless steel wires coated in nylon. Available in a variety of diameters (.010"-dia. to .036"-dia.) and in a range of qualities (7-strand to 49-strand), beading wire is mainly used for stringing beads.

Nylon bead thread

Bead thread is used when performing any of the various bead stitches and in bead embroidery.

Thread conditioner

A thread conditioner (such as Thread Heaven, beeswax, or synthetic beeswax) keeps the thread from fraying and protects it from water damage and decay.

Elastic or stretch cord

This stretchy material is easy to knot and is often used to make stretch bracelets without clasps.

FireLine

Originally developed for use only as fishing line, FireLine has come to be a common stringing material among bead weavers and produces strong, sturdy beadwork.

Chain

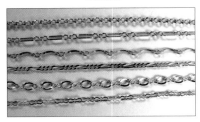

Chain is available in a number of sizes, styles, and finishes. It is used as a base for charm bracelets, as an extender at the end of a necklace, or just as a beautiful accent in jewelry pieces.

Hemp cord

Hemp cord is easy to knot, difficult to fray, and will hold its shape under normal pressure.

Leather cord

Leather cord is a strong, natural material that can be easily knotted and braided to add an organic look to a piece of jewelry.

Silk thread/cord

Silk thread/cord is easy to knot and is often used to string pearls and soft gemstones.

Satin cord

Satin cord is a smooth stringing material available in three sizes: bugtail (smallest diameter), mousetail, and rattail (largest diameter).

Natural fiber cords

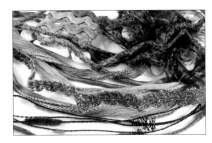

This type of stringing material is often used to add artistic interest and a mixed-media feel to a piece of jewelry.

Techniques

Crimping

Step 1: Slide a crimp bead onto the end of the stringing cord and then through one part of the clasp.

Step 2: Thread the cord back through crimp bead and the last bead you've added. Tug on the end of the cord so the crimp bead is between the last bead on the cord and the bead just before the clasp. There should be a little bit of slack so the clasp can flex when opened and closed, but there shouldn't be so much slack that the stringing cord is too visible.

Step 3: Crush the crimp by first gripping the crimp with the second groove in the crimping pliers (closest to the joint). Squeeze the pliers closed. Then, the crimp should be round on one side and indented on the other.

Step 4: Move the crimp to the first groove in the crimping pliers (closest to the tips). Firmly squeeze the pliers closed.

1.

2.

3.

4.

Wire Working

A note about wire gauge and hardness:
Wire used in jewelry making ranges from 10-ga. to 36-ga. The smaller the gauge number, the thicker the wire will be.

Dead-Soft wire is extremely flexible, malleable, and can be easily bent into any shape. It will not maintain its shape under stress.

Half-Hard wire is malleable like dead-soft wire, but it will maintain its shape under stress.

Full-Hard wire is tempered and will easily hold its shape under stress.

Opening and closing jump rings

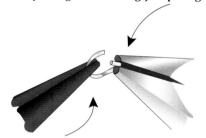

Use two pairs of chain nose pliers to open and close jump rings. Hold the upper edges of the jump ring near the opening; twist one plier towards you and twist the other away to open the jump ring. To close the jump ring, twist the pliers in the opposite direction to bring the ends back together. Never pull the jump ring ends out to the side, spreading it into an oval.

Making loops

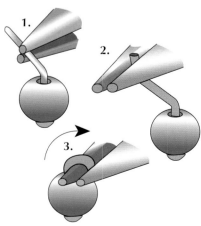

Grasp wire with the chain nose pliers and create a right angle bend, leaving a short tail. Use the round nose pliers to grab wire just past bend and twist to create a wire circle around the jaw of the pliers. **Note:** Vary the size of the loop by using different parts of the pliers (nearer the tip will create a smaller loop).

Wrapping loops

1.

Create a loop in a piece of wire, leaving extra length at each end. Hold one wire

2.

straight, and use chain nose pliers to wrap the second piece around the first wire below the loop. Tightly wrap as many times as desired and trim.

Making spirals

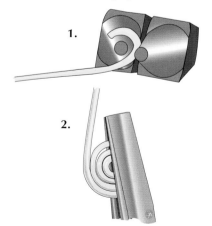

1.

2.

Form a loop with round nose pliers. Grasp the loop securely with chain nose pliers. Bend wire around initial loop with fingers, while turning pliers.

Bead Stitches

Abbreviations:
PT = pass through
PBT = pass back through

Stopper (tension) bead

A stop or tension bead is intended to keep loose beads from falling off and/or help hold tension. Do not count this bead as part of your project bead count. This bead is removed after enough beads have been added to anchor the thread. Leave a 6-in. tail to weave back through.

Pass through the stopper bead from right to left and then again from right to left. This anchors the thread without tying knots. *Note:* Stopper beads are shown in red on these pages.

Ladder stitch

Step 1: String through first bead, leaving a 4-in. tail. Go through a second bead, and then PT the first bead, from bottom to top. PT the top of second bead, out the bottom, and into the bottom of the third bead. Pull the thread out the top of the third bead, PBT the second bead (top to bottom), and up from the bottom of the third bead.

Step 2: Continue this pattern and PT every bead three times.

Step 3: After finishing the row, weave the thread back through each bead (see bolded line) for extra support.

Even-count flat peyote

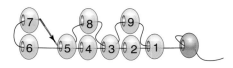

Step 1: Start with a stopper bead (shown in red). Then string on beads to the desired width.

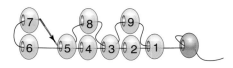

Step 2: Add bead 7, and go through bead 5. Add bead 8, and go through bead 3. Add bead 9, and go through bead 1.

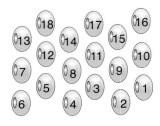

Step 3: Add bead 10, and go through bead 9. Add bead 11, and go through bead 8. Add bead 12, and go through bead 7. Continue this stitch until the desired length is achieved.

Brick stitch

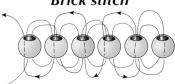

Step 1: *Base row:* No stopper bead is needed. Thread a needle, condition the thread, and string on two beads, leaving a 6" tail. PT both beads again, stitching in the same direction. Position the beads so they are side by side, and hold them so the thread is coming down through the second bead. Add a bead and PT the second bead from the top toward the bottom. PT the third bead from the bottom toward the top. Add the fourth bead and PT the third bead from the bottom up to the top. Then PT the fourth bead from the top through to the bottom.

Continue adding beads in this manner until the base row is the desired length. Then stitch back through the row in a zig zag manner to the beginning of the row. This strengthens the base row and will make it more stable to handle.

Step 2: Notice the threads that connect the beads across the top and the bottom of the base row. These threads are stitched under to attach the additional rows. String on two beads to start a new row. Pass the needle under the threads between the second and third bead from back to front (the needle slides under the threads to anchor the beads). Pull the thread snug. PT the second bead you just added on the second row from the bottom to the top. Add another bead. Pass the needle under the threads between the third and fourth bead from back to front. Pull the thread snug, and PT the new bead from the bottom to the top. Continue adding beads until you reach the end of the row.

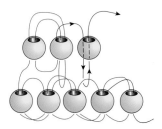

Step 3: Flip the beadwork piece around horizontally and work the next row from left to right, starting by adding two beads for the first row. When the beadwork is completed, weave in the tail and cut off excess thread.

Square stitch

Step 1: Add a stopper bead (shown in red). String on the desired width of beads. Add bead #8 and needle through bead #7 from right to left. Needle through bead #8 a second time, and add bead #9. After passing through bead #9 from left to right, secure by passing through bead #6 from right to left. Return through bead #9 from left to right. Continue adding beads in this manner.

Securing and adding threads

Securing a thread
End your thread when you have about 6 or 7 in. left. This gives you enough length to pass through several beads. It is always easier to end a thread with more thread length than you need, rather than too little.

Step 1: Pass through several beads on the edge of the beadwork, bringing the needle out of an up bead.

Step 2: Begin to pull the thread through the bead, but stop when there is about a 2-in. diameter loop. Insert the needle through the loop.

Step 3: Pull the needle and thread so the loop tightens up and the half hitch knot created slips up and into the beadwork. You can help the loop move along with the tip of your needle.

Step 4: Needle down through a couple more edge beads and add another half hitch knot. Repeat this for a third half hitch knot.

Step 5: Pull the thread taut and clip the excess with your wire cutters as close to the beadwork as possible. By pulling the thread taut, the end of the thread will disappear in between the beads.

Adding a new thread

1. Re-thread your needle and condition the thread. Pass through several beads in the area where you stopped stitching, and work your way to the spot where the next bead will be added. The more zigs and zags you add, the more secure your thread anchor is going to be.

2. Pull on excess thread tail that may be sticking out of the first bead you entered and cut it off very close to the beadwork.

Half-hitch knot

While holding bead fabric in left hand, pull thread up through a bead. Go under the base thread and back out, leaving a loop on the bottom side. Bring needle up through loop and slowly tighten. A double half-hitch simply brings the thread up through the loop twice.

Embroidery Stitches

Blanket stitch

Lazy-daisy stitch

Stem/split stitch

Running stitch

Knots

Overhand knot

Surgeon's knot

Tie a straight knot as in the first step of a square knot. Begin a second knot and wrap one thread through the loop three times, and then tighten. Refer to diagram at the bottom of first column.

Branch fringe

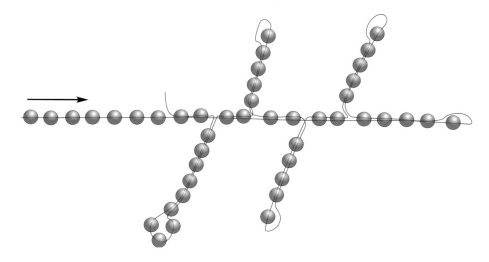

Short bead stack

Tall bead stack

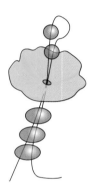

Picot stitch

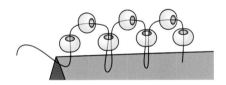

Fringe (on fabric)

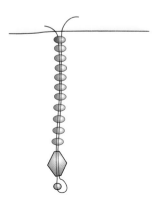

Crochet Stitches

Slip knot

Step 1: Make a pretzel shape with yarn. Insert hook as shown.

Step 2: Draw up loop, pulling down on both ends of yarn to tighten.

Slip stitch

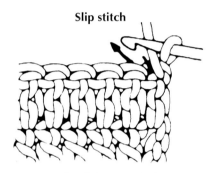

Step 1: Insert hook in next stitch.

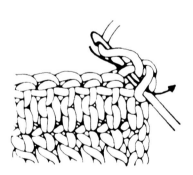

Step 2: Yarn over, draw yarn through stitch and loop on hook.

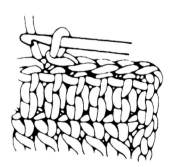

Step 3: Repeat from Step 1 for required number of stitches.

Sewing Guide

Single Needle Couching

Bring needle and knotted thread up through fabric. String on beads for line you wish to create. Working backwards, come up through fabric between bead 7 and 8 and bring needle over thread and back through fabric. Repeat between every few beads to secure in place.

Backstitch

Bring needle up through fabric. String on five beads. Go back through fabric and come up between bead 2 and 3. Pass back through beads 3,4, and 5 and repeat.

Whipstitch

With a needle and a doubled length of thread, pass through fabric from back to front, pass over (or through the edge of) item to be whipstitched (in this case, a fiber), and pass back into the fabric. Repeat down the length of the fiber.

Credits and Sources

Bead Adorned Knobs and Handles: Beading wire from Artistic Wire Ltd.; beads from The Beadery, Blue Moon Beads, Shipwreck Beads and Sulyn. Contact designer Barbara Matthiessen at barbaramatthiessen@earthlink.net.

Bead My Jeans!: Fall Flower Jeans: Fibers from EK Success; seed and bugle beads from Blue Moon Beads; disappearing ink marking pen from Dritz. Contact designer Lisa Swenson Ruble at lruble@allamericancrafts.com.

Bead My Jeans!: Ladders and Scallops Jeans: Beads from Create A Craft and Blue Moon Beads. Contact designer Dorothy Egan at degandesigns@aol.com.

Beaded Eyeglass Cases: Crystals from Swarovski; bugles from Mill Hill; seed beads from Toho Beads; fusible interfacing from Pellon; wool felt from National Nonwovens; suede from Ultrasuede; Silamide beading thread. Contact designer Linda Wyszynski at linda@hearthsidecreations.net.

Beaded Wine Glasses: Contact designer Nicole Campanella at beadwright@nicolecampanella.com.

Beads to Go!: Focal bead from Green Girl Studios; beads, wire, and findings from Beadalon. Contact designer Katie Hacker at katie@katiehacker.com; www.katiehacker.com.

Best Friend's Bracelet: Beading wire and crimp beads from Soft Flex Company. Contact designer Eleanore Macnish at emacnish@hotmail.com.

Black and White with a Dash of Red: Focal lampwork beads from Ellie Mac Design; secondary lampwork beads from Kennebunkport Bead Art; Nymo beading thread. Contact designer Lynda Musante at lsmusante@nifty-dev.com; www.niftydev.com.

Bohemian Mood Beading: Crystal clear protective spray coating from Krylon; dimensional decoupage glue, acrylic paint, and antiquing medium from Plaid; beads from The Beadery, Blue Moon Beads, Sulyn, and Shipwreck Beads; wire from Artistic Wire Ltd. Contact designer Barbara Matthiessen at barbaramatthiessen@earthlink.net.

Braided Cube Bracelet: Contact designer Lou Musante at lpmusante@niftydev.com.

Breezy Aqua Basket: Beads and shells from The Beadery; basket from Pier One Imports; fabric adhesive from Beacon Adhesives. Contact designer Mary Ayres at jmds@visuallink.com.

Build a Bead Button: Contact designer Kim Ballor at kballor@aol.com.

Christmastinis: Beads from Paula Radke Dichroic Beads; wire from Beadalon. Contact designer Paula Radke at paula@paularadke.com; www.paularadke.com.

Clever Conversations! Cell Phone Cases: Beads and crystals from Soft Flex Company; seed beads from Beyond Beadery. Contact designer Lisa Swenson Ruble at lruble@allamericancrafts.com.

Contrasting Tangents Embellished Neck Ring: Crystals from Swarovski, wire from Artistic Wire Ltd., Mini Twist 'n Curl tool by Soft Flex Company. Contact designer Lynda Musante at lsmusante@niftydev.com.

Copper Candlelight: Soft metal sheets and wire metal mesh from AMACO; foiled pressed beads from The Beadery. Contact designer Barbara Matthiessen at barbaramatthiessen@earthlink.net.

Delicate Lace Necklace: Berkley FireLine fishing line. Contact designer Alethia Donathan at dacsbeads@aol.com.

Desert Blue Bracelet: Connector buttons and closure from Fire Goddess, beading wire from Soft Flex Company. Contact designer Susan Barnes at susan@firegoddess.com; www.firegoddess.com.

Forget-Me-Not Necklace and Brooch: Wire and clasp from The Beadery; beads from The Beadery and Create A Craft. Contact The Beadery at info@thebeadery.com; www.thebeadery.com.

Grapetini Necklace and Earrings: Yarn from South West Trading Company; seed beads from Beyond Beadery. Contact designer Kelly Wilson at kellywilsondesigns@earthlink.net; www.kellywilsondesigns.com.

Jade With a Twist Necklace: Beads, wire, and findings from The Beadery. Contact The Beadery at info@thebeadery.com; www.thebeadery.com.

Jar Jewelry: Beads and wire from The Beadery; ribbon from Offray. Project designed for The Beadery at info@thebeadery.com; www.thebeadery.com.

"Lucies" Garden Bracelet: Nymo beading thread. Contact designer Kelli Burns at theholebeadshop@aol.com; www.theholebeadshop.com.

Luxurious Links: Crystals from Swarovski. Contact designer Beth Spicker at BethAnnDesigns@comcast.net.

Ocean Dreams Bracelet: Beading wire from Beadalon. Contact designer Katie Hacker at katie@katiehacker.com; www.katiehacker.com.

Off the Cuff Bracelet: All beads and supplies from The Bead Fetish. Contact designer Kim Fandry at beadfetish@sbcglobal.net.

Pearl Appeal Necklace: All beads and supplies from The Bead Fetish. Contact designer Kim Fandry at beadfetish@sbcglobal.net.

Peruvian Opal Bracelet: Contact designer Lynn Gifford at lrgifford@yahoo.com.

Raku Cascade Necklace: Beading wire from Soft Flex Company. Contact designer Lynda Musante at lsmusante@niftydev.com.

Rockin' Jewelry: Clear glaze from Krylon, wire from Artistic Wire Ltd. Contact designer Barbara Matthiessen at barbaramatthiessen@earthlink.net.

Savannah Flower Brooch: Contact designer Cynthy Anderson at cynthyan@earthlink.net.

School Spirit Bracelet: All materials from Fire Mountain Gems and Beads. Contact designer Laurel Musante at lemusante@niftydev.com.

Spring Green Dichroic Sparkle Set: Beads from Paula Radke Dichroic Beads; beading wire from Beadalon; crystals from Swarovski, Bali spacer beads from TierraCast Inc. Contact designer Paula Radke at paula@paularadke.com; www.paularadke.com.

True Fusion Necklace: Beads from Blue Moon Beads; crystals from Swarovski. Contact designer Nealay Patel at nealaysdesigns@gmail.com; www.nealaysdesigns.com.

Wheeler Reel Necklace: Beading wire and crimp beads from Soft Flex Company; beads from Halcraft USA. Contact designer Beth Wheeler at muttonhead@mchsi.com.

Wine Bottle Cape: Nymo beading thread. Contact designer Merit Cape at beadifull@gmail.com.

Notes ~ Inspirations ~ Ideas

Notes ~ Inspirations ~ Ideas

Designs